PRAISE FOR TOBY STANSELL AND *THE WINDING ROAD TO EXCELLENCE*

"The leadership concepts presented in this book are more than lessons learned through experience, they are truths to be followed. They are universal, timeless, and objective principles that worked yesterday, still work today, and will work tomorrow. They are easy to understand, have broad applicability, and (most importantly) are easy to put into practice. If you're looking to improve your day-to-day life as a leader, this book provides a well-defined framework for authentic leadership. And there's no better authentic leader than Toby Stansell to show you the way!"

SCOTT BRAND
Cofounder, Cargo

"Toby Stansell is a true leader who has the two most important characteristics that a real transformational leader can possess: strong, effective communication and a big heart! Toby believes in teamwork, best practice sharing, and leading by example. Toby makes those around him think, and achieve, more than they thought possible, and continually provide a vision of what can be. I am fortunate to be able to experience Toby's care and commitment as a friend and business associate. I recommend his book with great pleasure!"

RANDY DOBBS
Author, Transformational Leadership: A Blueprint for Real Organizational Change

"Toby Stansell is a wonderfully unique individual committed to doing the right thing, and backed up by a wealth of international experience, relationship building and a continuous desire to learn. We can all become better in business and as individuals by taking to heart what Toby has to say."

CRAIG BROWN

Owner & Chairman, Greenville Drive Minor League Baseball Team

"From my initial meeting with Toby, I knew he was an individual that I needed to spend time with to glean from his experience and partner with on transformational projects. One thing that definitely jumps out at you when you meet Toby is that he is incredibly young at heart! He is full of energy, dynamic, and willing to actively engage in development opportunities at various levels. He demonstrates a keen focus on leadership development and stands at the ready to impart his wisdom, all with the unique ability to weave his global exposure into his southern heritage."

BASIL O. DOSUNMU, CPA, CIA, C.M.

Chief Financial Officer, Capital Region Airport Commission | Richmond International Airport

"Things do not always go 'right' and rarely do they go as planned. Toby exemplifies the importance of positive thinking and adaptability as key aspects of leadership during periods of rapid change. He has instilled these traits in my everyday activities and is proof a smile goes a long way!"

SCOTT MOSS
Merger and Acquisition Executive

THE
WINDING
ROAD
TO
EXCELLENCE

THE
WINDING
ROAD
TO
EXCELLENCE

Leadership Lessons
Learned from Life's Potholes

G.T. "TOBY" STANSELL

Forbes | Books

Published by Forbes Books, Charleston, South Carolina.
Member of Advantage Media.

Forbes Books is a registered trademark, and the Forbes Books colophon is a trademark of Forbes Media, LLC.

Printed in the United States of America.

10 9 8 7 6 5 4 3 2

ISBN: 979-8-88750-005-8 (Hardcover)
ISBN: 979-8-88750-006-5 (eBook)

LCCN: 2022921790

Cover design by Matthew Morse.

This custom publication is intended to provide accurate information and the opinions of the author in regard to the subject matter covered. It is sold with the understanding that the publisher, Forbes Books, is not engaged in rendering legal, financial, or professional services of any kind. If legal advice or other expert assistance is required, the reader is advised to seek the services of a competent professional.

Since 1917, Forbes has remained steadfast in its mission to serve as the defining voice of entrepreneurial capitalism. Forbes Books, launched in 2016 through a partnership with Advantage Media, furthers that aim by helping business and thought leaders bring their stories, passion, and knowledge to the forefront in custom books. Opinions expressed by Forbes Books authors are their own. To be considered for publication, please visit **books.Forbes.com**.

This book is dedicated to my family: Susan, my wife, and our two children, Evyn and Taylor. While much of the content herein was crystallized from what I heard and learned while in the presence of many highly revered commercial, civic, and cultural leaders, my family has had to endure a lifetime of me repeatedly verbalizing, formalizing, and internalizing the principles that this book espouses. They had no choice but to listen regularly to the one-liners that formed the basis for the book, and even though I am sure they thought, "I've heard that one a thousand times already," they demonstrated enough grace to only roll their eyes and cover their ears on a few occasions. And without Susan's prodding and encouragement, over many years, I would never have engaged in this endeavor. They are the real heroes in the story, not me.

Contents

Part 2
Leadership Excellence: Lead from the Middle

Part 3
Organizational Excellence: Culture Trumps Strategy

Acknowledgments

My most sincere thanks go to the men and women who saw something in me that I did not know was there, who invested time and teaching in me when the results were not immediately obvious. I want to especially acknowledge Craig Brown and Randy Dobbs, true friends and colleagues in the latter stages of my career, who exposed me to elements of business and community service about which I was largely ignorant but which strengthened and revived in me the belief that we can all learn and do exceedingly more than we think. To Kacey Murphy and Scott Brand, Cargo's cofounders, thank you for giving me the opportunity to lead and grow one more company in the twilight of my career. In addition to my family, you two were the primary instigators of this book, as your persistent encouragement and financial investment in this project were the final pieces of the puzzle to make this a reality. To the individuals for whom I worked at every organization since I graduated from college, and you know who you are, thank you. Especially to my managers and colleagues when I served at IBM: that period of time was an inflection point for me, as the environment of friendly competition and the standard set by each and every one of you motivated me to develop the self-discipline and drive to perform in a manner that heretofore had been unimaginable and certainly unreachable. And lastly to my parents and my wife's parents. Neither shied away from confronting me when I made poor choices and behaved badly, even as an adult, and they always challenged me (and still do!) to set the right example, to do better, and to give more.

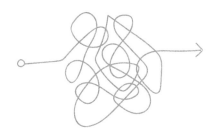

Prologue

LEADERSHIP LESSONS LEARNED FROM LIFE'S POTHOLES

Many of the principles, philosophies, and axioms you will encounter in this book did not originate with me. I have tried to give credit where credit is due. For many years I have said that I'm not sure that I have had an original thought in my entire life, but I have been fortunate to have spent time among many wise people. I have simply drafted in their wake and gleaned from them many of the proverbs and principles I have used to guide my life as a leader…and as a follower. This world needs more authentic leaders. Be one.

How this book came about is pretty simple. But that's true of some of the most important lessons that we learn throughout life. An everyday experience subtly impresses upon us an indelible truth that is universally applicable and infinitely valuable, but it doesn't dawn on us at the time that what just happened to us is going to repeat itself multiple times in multiple ways as we go through life. If we simply made it a priority to develop long antennas—to be alert to those experiences and to understand the gravity and importance of what we just encountered—we would realize the need to codify, internalize, and <u>write down</u> what we just learned because *we are going to need it again.* As much as we try to avoid any pain and suffering that we probably deserve when we make bad choices, decisions, and mistakes, it is exactly those circumstances that teach us the most and that force us to rethink and refine our belief structures, behaviors, and decision-making approaches so that we don't have to endure on a regular basis the ignominy and anguish that come with poor choices that hurt not only us but also our organizations, our colleagues, and those around us who love us the most, our friends and families.

The truth is, *we all tend to learn our most important lessons the hard way.*

When I was first approached about writing a book, those who were encouraging me were of the mindset that I should write a book that encapsulated my "recipe" for leadership and decision-making, a sort of mini handbook for leadership that captured and catalogued everything a person needed to know to get leadership "right," and if followed, would transform that individual into a great leader in short order. I quickly rejected that approach, as the market is flooded with how-to books that elevate the author to some godlike status, as if they had discovered the ultimate answer to some universal dilemma, question, or challenge that all humans face. I don't know how long the world has been here or how many years humans have been around, but one thing I do know is that nobody has fully figured out life. Even when we do know what to do, many times we simply won't—or

> **We all tend to learn our most important lessons the hard way.**

don't—do what we know to do. Generally, the problem is not a lack of knowledge; the problem is execution. And even though plenty have gone before us from whom we could easily learn how we should live and what we should do in most situations, we are all stubborn and have something in us that makes us want to do it our way.

So instead of penning a book that is delivered from the viewpoint that I have fully figured out life and leadership and what to do and how to do it, I would rather be honest and share some real-life stories of the things that I *didn't* get exactly right—in fact, situations that I got exactly wrong in some cases—that made an impression on me and that drove me to a resolute conclusion and decision that "I'm not doing *that* again!" This book is as much about what not to do as it is about finding a better way. At least for me, and I think this is true for many of us, we learn more from the potholes we drive into on old country roads than we do when we are smoothly sailing along the Autobahn in a 7 Series BMW or Mercedes S-Class. I've done a bit of both in my life, literally and figuratively, and the former experience usually provided the environments and venues where I learned principles and philosophies that made the biggest and longest-lasting impression on me. We don't have to bottom out in a pothole to learn a lesson that stays with us, but I can guarantee you that I have done more than my share of damage to personal and professional shock absorbers and suspensions! When we don't get something right the first time, when we are forced to navigate our way through something that is unfamiliar, when we are asked to do the hard thing and are not provided much direction but we find our way anyhow, those tend to be the moments that teach us the most and that we remember the longest. There's an old southern colloquial saying that communicates the reality of sometimes having to relearn an old lesson over again: "I knowed that, but I forgot it!" I don't want to repeatedly live out that reality in my own life, and I know you don't either.

Some of the potholes I've hit have been filled with rain and mud…and hurt. But I've always tried to learn something from every incident in life, especially the less than pleasant ones. It starts with being *willing* to learn, to know that I need help from others, that I don't hold all the knowledge or have all the answers. That perspective keeps me humble, makes me listen more intently to those around me, and makes me appreciate others' perspectives. We have to want to be better people and better leaders today than we were yesterday. Of course, if I encounter a pothole big enough to swallow an SUV on the route I take to work and I still hit it every day, then I haven't learned a thing, or worse yet, I don't *want* to, because I started from the position of "I'm right." Believing we are "right" is many times a leading indicator that we are self-centered and arrogant. Consciously or unconsciously holding such a perspective slows our pace of learning, makes us unapproachable, and keeps us from appropriately valuing the input and feedback offered by others, that if heeded, could make our lives, and our organizations, better.

There are plenty of us who, through no fault of our own, are encumbered with severe physical or mental challenges or illnesses that impact our ability to live a "normal" life. Beyond those challenges, however, my observations and experiences have led me to the conclusion that all of us are imbued with about the same number of assets and liabilities that we bring to life and leadership; it's just that yours are different from mine and mine are different from yours. What we do with them is what matters—that and how we transform into assets what on the surface appear to be liabilities, whether in business or in our personal lives. If we look at everything life hands us, good and bad, as an opportunity, we can begin to build a positive, principle-based framework for successful leadership. We are extraordinarily honored to have others put their trust in us and place us in positions of leadership. We are wise to be humble, careful, and considerate as to how we apply the influence our positions afford us to positively impact and hopefully make better the lives of those around us.

Much of this book is about sharing the lessons I've learned that have evolved into principles for how I want to lead my life and for how I want to lead organizations. It's a collection, of sorts, of ideas that have become signposts for me. I'm hopeful that a few of them might help you further refine your approach to life and leadership as well.

> If we look at everything life hands us, good and bad, as an opportunity, we can begin to build a positive, principle-based framework for successful leadership.

THE MANTRAS

In 2002, I was working as vice president of sales for a software company in Austin, Texas, when I was issued my first smartphone. It was a silver flip phone Palm Treo 300, and it had a raised keypad and was pretty elementary compared to what we have today. The funny thing about that phone, and maybe all palm 300s of that era as far as I know, is that they all had a spring with a limited life span that would break about every 300th time (maybe that's why it was called a Palm 300!) I would open the phone. Without warning, the hinge spring would fail, and the top of the phone would shoot across the room at about Mach 2, risking life and limb for everyone within fifty feet or so! But it *was* a smartphone, a device I could carry with me and into which I could key important points that I wanted to remember. I began to use the Notes application to record these short but salient principles and perspectives that were impressed upon me through circumstances that I was encountering. These usually took the form of one-liners that captured a lesson I'd learned or that reflected a learning experience in which I had willingly participated or grudgingly endured, as not all learning experiences emanate from pleasant circumstances. Many of them, as we all know, result from encounters with the potholes of life, if you will.

What I didn't know at first was that the notes I took on that phone were syncing with Microsoft Outlook. Even when I had to replace my phone on a regular basis, primarily because of a failed hinge and a missing top, and probably because I was moving too fast in trying to grow and mature the companies with whom I was engaged, it just never dawned on me that the notes on my phone were syncing with a software application on my laptop or a server somewhere. Remember, this was 2002, not 2022. I don't remember why or when I actually decided to open and use the Notes application in Outlook, but when I did, I got a real shock. I found that I had captured almost *eleven pages* of these one-liner lessons! After perusing a couple of pages and recalling the situations that spawned the (Aha!) moments that prompted me to record in a very concise fashion what I had learned, it dawned on me that, individually and collectively, what I had documented actually formed a framework for how to think about situations that we as human beings—not just businesspeople—encounter on a regular basis. I internally and informally began to refer to these little principles and philosophies as mantras for excellence, as at least in my own life, the collective framework for personal and business thought expressed by these mantras enabled me to perform as a human and as a leader in a more predictable, consistent, and effective manner. Most of these mantras were (and are) simple, but they conveyed some important foundational principles essential to being a person of character that I felt were helping me to become the kind of leader and person I wanted to be.

When I realized that I had accumulated eleven pages of these mantras, I began to segregate them into logical categories like sales excellence, personal excellence, corporate excellence, spiritual excellence, and other classifications of a similar sort. Over time, whenever I was offered the opportunity to speak at civic, commercial, and cultural events, I drew upon these notes I had been accumulating. When I had the opportunity to serve as the instructor for the Greenville, South Carolina, Chamber of Commerce's Minority Business Accelerator, at the time one of only six such entities in the country, I architected the initial curriculum and several of the courses with the mantras at their core. I turned to them again when I was a speaker for Clemson University's Center for Corporate Learning's Leadership Symposium and miniMBA program. The individuals enrolled in the courses I had the privilege to teach told me that they found the mantras memorable, compelling, and, best of all, relevant and useful in everyday situations. I was humbled that the individuals with whom I shared these mantras found them relatable, easy to recall and apply, and effective, which is the ultimate test of worth for me. I'm glad that's been the case, and I hope it can be for you.

THE RACONTEUR

I enjoy telling stories. Storytelling is in my family's DNA. Growing up, either while fishing or sitting on the front porch waiting for the rain to clear in order to go fishing, I listened to the stories my father, my uncles, and their contemporaries told. Honestly, they would tell some of the funniest stories you've ever heard in your life. It's kind of a lost term these days, but in the South, gifted and engaging storytellers like my dad and uncles historically were referred to as "raconteurs," individuals skilled at spinning colorful and amusing yarns that could keep an audience spellbound for hours. Almost all of those stories are humorous in some shape, form, or fashion, but many also have a serious point behind them. My dad is that kind of storyteller, although he is now in the twilight of his life and does not recall things quite as readily and crisply as he once did. He's sort of like a living embodiment of the old E. F. Hutton commercial—when Pop speaks, people listen. He was always coming up with a pearl of wisdom, packaged in just a few words, and the way he said it hit you between the eyes because you realized just how applicable and how true it was.

I can't put myself in the same category as my dad or my uncles, but I frequently introduce my perspectives and principles of leadership by sharing the stories of the situations and circumstances that spawned them or ways that I have applied them in my own life or business. So you will encounter some stories here. I hope some will make you laugh. Mostly I hope some will make you think. That's how we learn, for stories don't require us to hypothesize or visualize a particular situation or setting; they actually take us back to a concrete, personally experienced, historical situation that the raconteur can share with passion and conviction because they *lived it*. Stories are not abstract; they are real. And they prompt us to recall similar situations that we have encountered and enable us to better connect to our own experiences. It's the reason that when someone tells a good story, those who listened want to share their own stories as well.

THE MANTRAS, THE RACONTEUR, AND THE PURSUIT OF EXCELLENCE

I am really sheepish about saying this, as I hate ego, arrogance, and self-promotion, but the one-liners that I had coined and used regularly in my presentations or speeches began to take on a life of their own. My colleagues and contemporaries, at least locally, began to refer to the mantras as Tobyisms. I have never called them that, as the focus needs to be on the principles they represent and not on the author, so I hope that moniker is just a confirmation that the hearer or reader remembered a few of the mantras and that they were successful in adapting and applying them in ways that allowed them to put the ideas to work in their own lives and enterprises. I hope they will resonate with you as well, which is why I have assimilated many of them in this book.

When I started accumulating the mantras for excellence that serve as the foundation of this book in the Notes application on my first smartphone, I had no intention of ever sharing any of them with a broader audience in a publication of any sort. I certainly didn't have any designs on writing a book! I didn't record the mantras in any particular order. They were thoughts that came randomly as reactions and responses to all types of situations and experiences, moments where I'd found my way through the woods and realized that I had just discovered something worth remembering. So there is certainly no hierarchy or order among the mantras. I hope that you will find ways to apply in your life and in your business the ones that resonate with you. In fact, I encourage you to read them in any order you wish and to come back to those that register—those that stick. My experience is that the mantras I share here will work in any situation that you encounter—they worked yesterday, they work today, and they will work tomorrow—and they don't unfairly disfavor or favor anyone because of the size of the company they work for or because of their color, race, creed, experience, or education. In short, I have done my best to make sure that the mantras meet the test of being universal, timeless, and objective.

The mantras are only effective to the degree that they are easily understood, transferable concepts and principles that have broad applicability and are easy to put into practice. I hope that you will find them easy to grasp and apply in experiences you encounter and in your day-to-day life as a leader…and as a follower. I encourage you to pick ones that resonate with *you* and then adapt them to your own language, apply them to your own needs, and carry them out in your own style. Not every mantra will resonate with you or be relevant or important to every reader. That is okay, as that is the way it should be, for we are all different. That being said, I do hope you find several here that you can put to practical use. What the mantras do is propel us to architect a well-defined set of philosophies and approaches—a personal framework—of our own, to examine our perspectives, platforms, and priorities as leaders so that what we think and discover and promote will draw out the best in those around us. One great thing about the mantras is that they can be—should be—adapted and applied in a leadership style and decision-making approach that is consistent with your own experiences, expertise, talents, and personality so that you remain comfortable in your own skin. You don't have to be something or somebody you're not, but you do have to commit to becoming the best you, and the best leader, you can be. Anything less puts each of us in the category of being an also-ran, a participant on the leadership landscape but not a champion, not a long-term influencer, not a difference maker, not a changemaker, not a transformational leader whose influence will make a *significant* positive impact long after you have retired and even after you have departed this life. The immutable truth is that a consistent pattern of decision-making increases the level of trust placed in you by those surrounding you and expands your sphere of influence. If you will "burn the mental calories" and invest the effort to review, learn, adopt, and adapt these mantras in a way that is consistent and congruous with your particular situation and needs, you *will* be a better leader. It is my hope that the principles and approaches shared in this book will become a shorthand reference that equips you to communicate the ideals, values, and approaches to those who are within the sound of your voice and that they become the proof points for the type of leader you want—and purport—to be.

MANTRAS FOR EXCELLENCE:

O Authentic living precedes authentic leadership.

O You get extra points for plagiarism.

O Your greatest weakness is often an unprotected or misguided strength.

O Relish the state of ignorance.

O My legacy of leadership is not what I do or accomplish, but what others become, do, or accomplish as a result of any influence I have in their lives.

O If you work with me, position, pedigree, and privilege mean nothing; performance means everything.

O The biggest difference between people who do and people who don't is that people who do simply believe they can.

THE FOUNDATION: WHO YOU ARE VERSUS WHAT YOU DELIVER

In 1982, I was still in the middle of an eighteen-month sales training program as a new hire for IBM. In a fashion that was altogether out of keeping with IBM tradition, I never completed my IBM education process, as after nine months at the company, I was provided the unique opportunity to lead my own sales territory based out of Asheville, North Carolina. It was a territory focused on large manufacturers, and my biggest account was a company whose IT department was under the leadership of a gentleman named Dick Holdredge. I was about as green as they come. I knew nothing about the computer industry and had been hired because I had a background in manufacturing, not information technology. Mr. Holdredge, on the other hand, was a seasoned and experienced IT executive, and the company, head-quartered in Europe, was a massive manufacturer with six operating units in America. I hadn't been the territory representative for more

THE WINDING ROAD TO EXCELLENCE

than a few months when I was called into Mr. Holdredge's office. He wasted no time putting me in my place. He said, "Toby, do you know what's expected of a real IBM rep? You need to be familiar with every relevant IBM product and service. I expect you to know 'em backward and forward, to figure out which ones are relevant to my business, to share with me and to share with my staff whether we've got a dollar to spend or not so that we know what IBM's introducing." He lit me up for forty-five minutes. When he wound down, he said, "Toby, do you know that you're the worst IBM rep I've ever had?" He held up the annual IBM customer satisfaction survey that had been lying on his desk. "When I send this in, hopefully you will get taken off this account, and I will get a *real* IBM account representative." He went through all the customer satisfaction rankings relative to his assigned IBM sales representative…me. He had given me the lowest score in every ranking. "Now," he said, "I want you to get out of my office. Hopefully, I won't have to deal with you for much longer."

I'd never felt so low. I knew what he had said was true. I had been successful before coming to IBM, successful enough that I had let the assignment of being an IBM account representative go to my head, and I thought I was "important." I wasn't working nearly as smartly or as hard as I needed to. I was not doing or giving my best. I quickly arrived at the conclusion that Mr. Holdredge was right and that soon I would be reassigned, demoted, or worse, fired, but what he'd told me struck such a strong chord that I set about trying to learn everything I could about this industry that was so new to me. I busted my rear end to do everything I could to support and lead my nine customers but especially the company for which Mr. Holdredge worked. About ninety days after Mr. Holdredge had lit into me, I went into the branch office for a meeting with my manager to review the customer satisfaction surveys that my clients had submitted. As my marketing manager went through my customers' survey rankings, he came to Mr. Holdredge's review. Completely unexpected by me, the results that the marketing manager read from Mr. Holdredge's survey were surprisingly positive across the board, including his review of my performance as his assigned IBM sales representative. My only thought was, "I have no idea how this happened, but somehow Mr. Holdredge's survey got mislabeled, and I am going to have to tell my boss and Mr. Holdredge what has happened." So I asked my marketing manager if he was sure that he had the correct survey for Mr. Holdredge, and he unequivocally stated yes.

After the review was finished, I drove back up the mountain from Greenville, South Carolina, to Asheville, North Carolina, where I lived and worked. I called Mr. Holdredge's assistant the next day (this was before cell phones) and was successful in securing an appointment a day later. I went to his office that day and shared with him, "Mr. Holdredge, there's been some kind of mix-up. You read in front of me the poor marks you assigned to me on your customer satisfaction survey, but when I had my performance review, the results my marketing manager shared with me were not the same. The only conclusion that I can come to is that they got your survey mixed up with someone else's."

Mr. Holdredge looked at me and said, "No, Toby, that's not what happened. When I called you into my office, I knew you hadn't been doing this job long. I had a few weeks before the deadline to return that survey. I chewed you up one side and down the other. But," he said, "let me tell you what happened. It was apparent to me by the change in your behavior and your attention to our account that you were doing everything you could to learn what I expected from you. You learned about our company and what we needed and could benefit from. You invested the time to learn the solutions that IBM has to offer its customers and paid attention to what I needed. You've become a different salesperson, so I changed my responses before I returned the survey. You learned what it takes to be a real IBM sales representative."

Dick Holdredge made me do what I didn't have the maturity or discipline to do myself. He pushed me to do what I could—but wouldn't—do. That's a lesson I've never forgotten. It took someone else to hold that mirror up, but I looked at my reflection and did my best to adjust and to improve. The truth is, I adjusted out of fear. I was afraid of looking stupid in front of my IBM peers, I was afraid of being a failure, and I was really afraid of losing my job, because at that time, I was the sole breadwinner in our family. Today, I count Dick Holdredge as one of a very small handful of business colleagues—customers, bosses, and peers—who cared enough to be tough on me in a way that significantly impacted my commitment and performance as a professional and altered the direction and trajectory not only of my career but also of my life.

That lesson is a cornerstone for a number of related concepts that form the core of this book. If there is a pattern or a foundation among the mantras, it's this: You've got to start by figuring out who you are. How do you see yourself? What are your personal values? How does your mind work? What sort of leader do you want to be? The leader you want to be starts with the person you are. One of the mantras you will encounter in the book is this one: Authentic living precedes authentic leadership. I didn't coin that phrase. I read it somewhere and it stuck with me. But it's perfect, and you can't improve upon perfection. So I adopted it. As I heard someone say one time—and educators hate this—you get extra points for plagiarism. Why invent something that is already out there in the public domain, ideally expresses a profound truth, and *works*?

If you can be honest about how you see yourself, then you have to be honest about how you see others. How do you treat people? Do you see others as people who can expand your mind and enlarge your life? As sources of experiences and knowledge different from your own? Do you appreciate people for the risks they are brave enough to take, or do you judge them when they fail? Do you think people are likely to rise when given the chance, or do you keep watch, waiting for them to fall? Where you land on those kinds of questions will shape everything about how you lead and will determine whether others want to work with you and for you for the long term. Anybody can fool somebody for a brief period of time, but in the long run, your true colors will show themselves. You can't act out what you think a leader ought to be or do; it has to be real.

> The leader you want to be starts with the person you are.

In my own case, I often say, "If you've known me for only five minutes, you know me." I don't pretend to be someone I am not, and I am not going to surprise you by saying or doing something that runs counter to what I believe and who I am. If I do that, then I owe the individual who witnesses that failure a sincere apology that I have not acted in a way that is consistent with the principles that I espouse. My hope is that the things that matter to me—humility, demonstrating sincere interest in you, and the values of integrity and credibility—are palpable and obvious from our first meeting, for they are not intended to be fleeting characteristics that vaporize over time. There are some nonnegotiables in life—what you believe and how you behave relative to faith, family, and friendships. Put a wall around these things and deal with them according to your core belief structure. This foundation will be the resource from which you draw all your strength. Everything else? It's all on the table and up for negotiation with a purview toward personal and professional growth, change, and improvement. Except for the nonnegotiables, we can't hold on to anything too tightly or too long. We live in an incredibly dynamic, fast-paced, and rapidly changing world. In many cases, the things we were right about yesterday, we may be dead wrong about today.

Once we've taken an honest stock of ourselves and of how we see others and the changing world around us, and we have defined those things in our lives that are off-limits and nonnegotiable, do we believe that we've already learned all we are capable of knowing, or do we see learning as a lifelong journey? Do we see ourselves as having come ashore or as never having arrived? Do we behave as if we have been elected or perpetually running for office?

If you believe you've got the absolute, sure-fire right answer, then the moment you turn your back and walk smugly away, your "right" answer starts to erode as the best solution. Because if you are certain that you have all the right answers, then your self-assessment better include the adjective *arrogant*. Your ego will get in the way of your own success. The actual truth is that many times, your greatest weakness is an unprotected or misguided strength. Aside from things illegal, immoral, and unethical, we should embrace life and learn to have a natural intellectual curiosity and appreciation for *everything* we might encounter. We're all a product of our upbringing and our experiences, but instead of remaining in the comfort and confines of those experiences and closing ourselves off from other beliefs, experiences, and thought processes, we should be looking for and open to new opportunities to learn.

Our willingness to realize that we can't wait for underperformance, failure, our customers, our competition, or the market to push us to change or improve is one of the criteria that will make us voracious learners and better leaders. For generations before us, our ancestors—even my parents' generation—were taught to *resist* change. For the last several decades, we have been implored and taught to *embrace* change. That approach is too slow today. We have to proactively *look* for change so that we can identify new emerging opportunities and then have the good judgment to be able to discern between fads and true trends. Fads are short lived, so we need to reject those, but we must examine the trends to determine which ones are worthy of our attention and resources and on which we can capitalize by being a first mover or an early adopter of a market change that presents significant commercial, economic, social, or civic opportunity. Most shifts of this nature may not be obvious to the naked eye or casual observer. Inherent in every good leader is the willingness to learn and change, not by simply learning something new or doing something different but by learning and doing something *better*.

We must learn to say yes to legitimate opportunities, even when we are not sure we know everything we need to know to take advantage of the situation. Not knowing all the answers is not a reason to hold in place. How often have you not taken action on something because you were afraid of failing or afraid you were going to look stupid in front of your peers or superiors? Not knowing all the answers and having to feel your way for a bit is not a synonym for failure. We can learn to relish the state of ignorance when we teach ourselves not to be embarrassed or insecure because we don't know something. My dad has a great saying: "You need to learn the difference between stupidity and ignorance. Stupidity is fatal. Ignorance, on the other hand, is curable." Seen this way, not knowing isn't a liability; it's an opportunity.

Knowing how we see ourselves, how we see others, and how we view opportunities for learning offers the origin for several of the mantras I will discuss in the early sections of this book. I start by acknowledging a key awareness: Who you are is more important than what you do. Results matter; in fact, it's all about the results, but we must realize that we cannot drive organizations that create great results if we don't exhibit high character at every step of the journey. Our character must be fully installed and front and center before driving and measuring performance. Thinking this way recognizes real performance as the positive impact we make in other people's lives. You'll learn plenty about me—good and bad—over the course of this book, but if you asked me to sum up who the real Toby Stansell really is, I'd say it this way: my legacy of leadership, especially at this stage in my life and career, is not what I do or accomplish but what others become, do, or accomplish as a result of any influence I have in their lives.

Learning the mantras that guide me didn't always come easily. Sometimes I was my own worst enemy. Even formulating what I wanted to be my legacy of leadership came only with time and experience and, sometimes, having someone else show me myself with such clarity that I had to look in the mirror a bit differently.

A lot of the mantras reflect a mirrored image of the expected in as much as they take frequently held conventional positions about the qualities of good leadership and they turn them around, kind of like how the backward lettering of ECNALUBMA looks quite identifiable in your rearview mirror as the word AMBULANCE when you need to get out of the way. Because we live in such a rapidly changing, dynamic world, as I alluded to earlier, I think it is imperative that we test and challenge convention. Just because something has been done a certain way for a long time doesn't make it right, especially today. We also tend to get caught up in what is seen as popular. I don't care anything about achieving popularity—I want to be liked, same as the next person, but I want people to like me because they like the authentic me, not a facade me that is on display simply to fit in or to avoid drawing unnecessary attention to my differences. Substance always trumps style. Even the most talented people you encounter cannot perform to their potential and generate maximum results until they transform their talent into applicable skills and apply those skills in the right way. Possessing encyclopedic knowledge in itself means little if you can't turn knowledge into tools you can put to use. I have translated this perspective into a mantra that I have used to shape organizational culture, and that mantra is this: if you work with me, position, pedigree, and privilege mean nothing; performance means everything.

The kind of thinking that has produced these mantras of excellence arises from a belief that we all have the capacity to be better versions of ourselves. The very first mantra I ever wrote down remains a centrally important one to me, so important that I'm going to come right back to it in the first chapter of the book: The biggest difference between people who do and people who don't is that people who do simply believe they can. How do you transfer that belief into a will to act on it? Leaders are people who believe they can, then they decide they will, and then they find a way.

Of course, a mantra is, by definition, something that is intended to be repeated, and the very origin of the word from the Sanskrit is "a thought behind speech or action," so as you find some mantras that work for you and adapt them to your own words and world, I hope that they become shorthand instruments for your own repeatable actions and for the philosophies, principles, and actions you hope to foster and inspire in others.

Leaders are people who believe they can, then they decide they will, and then they find a way.

PART 1

PERSONAL AND PROFESSIONAL EXCELLENCE: PEOPLE WHO DO

MANTRAS FOR EXCELLENCE:

O   Never say no to an opportunity because you are afraid.

O   Real freedom is not being able to do anything you want to do. Real freedom is having the power to do what you know you ought to do.

O   Stop trying to draw attention and start paying attention.

O   Humility is more important than visibility.

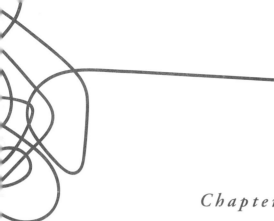

Chapter 1

NEVER GIVE IN TO FEAR

My third job out of college was designing and selling material handling systems for Engineered Products in Greenville, South Carolina, a company my dad had done business with for years. I'd come to it after a couple of brief professional stints selling business forms and then Toyota forklifts. At Engineered Products, I liked the work, and I came to know and like the sales manager, who was something of a legend in our industry. Shortly after going to work there, I also got to know the owner and president a little bit, and I liked him as well. As a young salesperson, my customers were gracious, and almost to a person, they readily embraced me. I was comfortable. Okay, the truth was I was so comfortable that I carried forward from my collegiate days an attitude and work ethic of doing enough to perform well, but I certainly didn't push myself. Although standard operating hours were 8:30 a.m. to 5:00 p.m., I usually arrived at work a little before nine, and I didn't work as hard as I could have. In fact, I had two side businesses that competed for my attention. I had begun repairing and ultimately making fishing rods when I was in high school, and in college I began selling stereos to a number of students on campus. I didn't make enough money from these businesses to support my wife and me, but they were a lot of fun, and the businesses grew because I took good care of my customers, and many of them referred me to their friends and colleagues. I was successful in designing and selling storage rack and conveyor systems and meeting my sales quotas, but I was really just coasting—you know, gliding along, knowing inside that I was being successful by relying on my personality and my innate ability to connect with people and convince them to act, which, for a salesperson, meant that they were placing orders.

One day a gentleman from my church, Vernon McCurry, approached me. He knew about my sales background. He told me that he was with IBM. He said, "I would like for you to come interview with us."

Now I'd never touched a computer outside of a required programming class I'd taken in college where I had learned to write very elementary Fortran programs by keying them into eighty-column punch cards using an IBM Model 129 Card Data Recorder. I didn't even know what the letters IBM stood for! I respected Mr. McCurry, so when he told me that IBM needed people who understood manufacturing and had sold into the manufacturing industry, I humored him and agreed I would interview with the branch manager and one of the marketing managers in IBM's Greenville, South Carolina, office. I was so ignorant about IBM that I didn't know IBM employees wore—every day without fail—a kind of corporate uniform consisting of a navy or gray suit, a white shirt, and a yellow or red tie. I showed up for my interview in a loud plaid sport coat, blue shirt, and no tie. To an IBMer, I must have looked like some yahoo off the street with no sense of professional decorum. I obviously was a little out of my element, yet the interview lasted for more than six hours.

Looking back, I believe that the interview went on so long and I was introduced to so many people because they appreciated the fact that I had an entrepreneurial spirit, I knew how to sell and sell myself, and I showed no fear, even though I didn't fit the mold of a prospective IBM employee. The truth is, I didn't know enough about the legacy IBM culture to know I should have been embarrassed, or even worse, afraid of being rejected.

To my surprise, IBM made me a job offer, and to be honest, I did my best to ignore it and to act like it would just go away. I liked what I was doing, and I knew I had it pretty easy. A week or so after the interview, the IBM marketing manager had left me a message at home, and I hadn't returned his call. Frankly, and I am embarrassed to admit this today, I was being disrespectful and rude. The truth is that I was afraid to say yes to a job that presented an incredible realm of possibilities but that was in an industry I knew nothing about. I may not have shown it on the outside, but the opportunity scared me on the inside. A week or so after receiving the offer, I traveled to Greensboro, North Carolina, to work on a large textile warehouse project where I was designing a storage rack and conveyor system. When I returned home from Greensboro in the early evening, my wife, Susan, said that Pete Delle Donne from IBM had called and really needed to know if I was going to accept their offer. Sheepishly, I told Susan that IBM was just too big of a company for me. I probably offered a dozen other excuses. "I think I'm just going to stay where I am," I told her.

Now my wife is one of the most intuitive, insightful people I have ever encountered, and she knows me better than anyone. Susan said to me, "Toby, if you're going to turn down this opportunity because you're scared, that's a poor excuse." Susan can be quite persuasive without trying. I took the job. Doing so changed the direction and trajectory of my entire career. With Susan's help, I learned a lesson

THE WINDING ROAD TO EXCELLENCE

that has never left me: never say no to an opportunity because you are afraid.

My early time at IBM wasn't without its bumps, as you know from the story I shared in the introduction when my customer, Dick Holdredge, told me I was a terrible salesperson. However, nine months into my training program, a process that typically lasts a year and a half, IBM branch leadership asked if I was interested in assuming responsibility for a key account sales territory based out of Asheville, North Carolina, that had been vacated by someone being promoted. The territory was comprised primarily of large manufacturing companies. One of the requirements of the position was that I would have to move my family from Greenville to Asheville so that I lived in the Asheville territory and was part of the community. The reason that this role was even offered to me was because none of the more experienced account representatives in the Greenville branch would agree to move to Asheville. I am pretty sure I was the last resort—the bottom of the barrel. But I was at least astute enough to recognize a unique opportunity, as it was not lost on me that most sales representatives at IBM didn't get an opportunity for a key account sales territory until they had put in five or six successful years on the job. I went home and talked to Susan, and once again we said yes.

Despite nearly getting fired by my biggest customer, once I faced the music and learned the business, by my third year that territory had become the number one revenue-producing territory in the Greenville branch of the National Marketing Division. Had I given in to fear, I may never again have had the chance to learn how to become a professional sales executive. My fear of failure and fear of looking stupid helped me transform from a "professional" who didn't work very hard and lacked self-discipline to someone who acted upon internalized incentives. I grew from someone who was externally motivated to someone who was intrinsically driven. I have come to learn that the most valid test of maturity for any individual is the ability to be self-managed—in other words, you do not need extrinsic motivation to do what you know needs to be done. Someone shared with me one time, "Real freedom is not being able to do anything you want to do. Real freedom is having the power to do what you know you ought to do."

I learned to become self-managed not because it was a trait I was born with but because Dick Holdredge was smart enough to give me a chance to prove his initial assessment of me was wrong. Maybe he saw that I was the sort of person who did not want to disappoint him. Or maybe he saw that people can grow into who they are capable of becoming. He gave me the opportunity to learn humility. I wasn't the smartest person in the room. I didn't have the purest or most obvious talent. His actions were essential to me discovering the real freedom that awaited me.

The most valid test of maturity for any individual is the ability to be self-managed.

That discovery in turn was directly linked to Susan's wise advice that put me in the position in the first place, to never pass up opportunity because of fear. Once I embraced that approach to life, it helped my confidence grow, but not in some overt, "Look at me!" center-of-attention fashion. Real confidence is not braggadocious, self-aggrandizing, or attention-grabbing. In fact, two of my most important mantras speak to the kind of quiet leadership that ultimately develops people to their full potential and helps lead an organization to achieve extraordinary results. Those two mantras are *stop trying to draw attention and start paying attention* and *humility is more important than visibility*. I can't honestly tell you if the quiet confidence that was being developed in me was newly found or resurrected from challenges I had faced and risks that I'd taken earlier in life but to which I hadn't given a lot of thought. Confidence didn't create false bravado in me, and it didn't produce a big ego; in fact, it did somewhat the opposite: It allowed me to see that the fear of looking stupid was actually… stupid. It allowed me to be less afraid of making mistakes. And it definitely led me to wholeheartedly believing in that first mantra I ever wrote down: The biggest difference between people who do and people who don't is that people who do simply believe they can. By refusing to give in to fear, I had developed the confidence to believe that as long as I accurately estimated what was at stake, the worst thing that might happen to me is that I could end up being wrong or looking silly. The wrong choice or mistake would not be of such a magnitude that I (or my team and company) could not recover. In the process I learned that what is really important is to find a new way to do the thing that didn't work. I believed that I could find solutions to problems. I believed that I could help people work toward common ends. I believed that I could learn new things. Because of the strength of that belief, I have learned that the key to success many times is to simply buckle down and find a way. We may not always take the easiest, most efficient, or most elegant path to accomplish a task or achieve the desired objective, but we *will* find a way.

> I have learned that the key to success many times is to simply buckle down and find a way.

MANTRAS FOR EXCELLENCE:

O All of us possess about the same number of assets and liabilities; some people's assets and liabilities are just more noticeable than others.

O "If you can't have what you want, you better learn to want what you have. 'Cause if you don't, you'll be miserable." —Hunter Park

O It's okay to be competitive, but don't be comparative.

O Turn what most people would consider a liability, whether in business or in life, into an asset.

O "Everyone is a potential winner. Some people are disguised as losers. Don't let their appearance fool you." —Ken Blanchard

O "We make a living by what we get. We make a life by what we give." —Winston Churchill

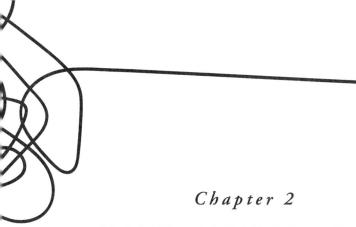

Chapter 2

MAKING THE MOST OF
WHAT YOU HAVE

Where does this internal strength come from? I absolutely do not believe it's because of some innate talent or ability that makes any of us special or better than others. I can guarantee you that I'm not special. The closest thing that ever set me apart from others isn't exactly the kind of thing anyone with good sense would ask for: I was born with a hole between two of the chambers of my heart. My mom always told me that the hole was the size of a dime, but that claim may have been more for effect than for accuracy. It's called an atrial septal defect, which meant there was a hole in the wall between the upper chambers of my heart. One result of my condition was that I was always small for my age. My sister weighed thirty pounds when she was two years old; I weighed thirty-six pounds when I entered the first grade! It meant that I was somewhat more prone to respiratory infections, and I certainly wasn't the first person chosen in a game of kickball. Let's face it: I was a runt.

I was born in Oak Ridge, Tennessee, and spent my first eight years there before we moved to Memphis. In Tennessee, you could enter first grade as long as you were six years old on or before December 31. I was born on December 15, so not only was I smaller than my class-mates, I was also younger. I never looked at my comparatively small size as a physical liability, but I was intent on keeping up with my peers, mentally and physically, in the classroom, on the playground, and on the ball field. I just figured I had to find some new ways to be competitive—and to win. I could never have articulated it as a child, but I think way back then I was beginning to form the belief that everybody has about the same number of assets and liabilities. They're just different. Some people's liabilities are more visible than others. But if you focus on thinking of them as liabilities, then you form a victim's mentality, which is one of the worst perspectives you can hold. *Never play the victim.*

My mother had a simple but brilliant way of illustrating what I mean. She made us appreciate what we had rather than focus on what we might be missing. She would say, "Let me tell you something. If you got a group of twenty people together in a room and asked each of them to anonymously write down their worst problem, something that nobody outside their immediate family knew about or even imagined, then have them crumple up the paper, throw it in a pile with the other nineteen pieces of paper, and mix them all up, then ask each person to pick out one note containing one individual's most closely held secret and worst problem and silently read what someone else is facing, in almost every case, you would want your own problem back." We are always tempted to believe that other people have it better than we do. The truth is, we don't have a clue what other people are facing or have faced. Too often we want to compare ourselves to others and then build excuses. "I don't have the same educational pedigree as them." "I didn't come from money like they did." "Nobody gave me the same opportunities." A former boss of mine and one of seven men who had a profound influence on my life, Hunter Park, once told me, "Toby, if you can't have what you want, you better learn to want what you have, 'cause if you don't, you'll be miserable."

Contemplating Hunter Park's advice and drawing upon my mother's insight, I learned that when you compare yourself to others, the result is either going to boost your ego or it's going to make you jealous. Neither one is a healthy or endearing trait. There's an old southern saying: the reason the grass looks greener on the other side of the fence is because it's probably growing on top of a septic tank. The conclusion I came to was that it's okay to be competitive, but don't be comparative.

When I was eleven years old, I still weighed only seventy pounds. I saw heart specialists regularly, and they monitored my condition, but open-heart surgery was more of a rarity in those days, and the doctors knew that sometimes the hole repaired itself. Then, over the summer between sixth and seventh grade, I gained twenty pounds. Talk about a transformation! Twenty pounds in twelve weeks. It turns out that the hole in my heart had healed on its own. I was pronounced a "normal" kid again. The thing is, I always saw myself as normal; I just knew that sometimes I had to work harder to accomplish what I wanted or needed to achieve.

I used to give a presentation about the qualities of good leaders and the way we can build teams, and I opened the presentation by joking that if I ever wrote a book, I'd title it *What Not to Do*. Well, that title didn't stick, as you can tell, but I'd pick on myself for a bit in the introductory part of the presentation and share things about myself that fit the bill of "things not to do in order to be successful," such as "Don't be born with a hole in your heart." Then I went on to say it was probably wise not to be born in the town where they developed the technology behind one of the two atomic bombs that brought the curtain down on World War II, and I would share my story of growing up in Oak Ridge. It made for a good joke, and most people probably wouldn't look to sign on for a place with such a legacy or where, as government employees in what was intended to be a temporary factory town, all the housing consisted of either dorm-style buildings for young single workers or identical nine-hundred-square-foot houses for families. Those flat-roofed houses were made out of cinderblock and featured little or no insulation. In East Tennessee, summers are hot and humid. For entertainment, I used to take a screwdriver and carve out the concrete between the cinder blocks so I had a spyhole through which I could peer outside. It wasn't exactly living in paradise, but there were other realities about Oak Ridge that made it a pretty amazing place to be a kid.

Oak Ridge was home to the Manhattan Project, the government-sanctioned initiative to create a weapon that would bring an end to World War II. It was a place subject to secrecy and where everyone from janitors to nuclear engineers were essentially treated the same. One immutable rule for everyone who worked in Oak Ridge was this: "Don't tell anyone what goes on inside." The funny thing was, before the first atomic bomb was dropped on Hiroshima in the Second World War, almost nobody working in the Oak Ridge facilities actually knew what they were building! The various operations were segregated across the multiple plants, and each employee had a very limited view of the work being performed. In such an age of relative innocence, the only prevailing theme around which all the workers rallied was, "We're helping our boys win the war!" My, how times have changed.

In Oak Ridge, all the employees, no matter which contractor or agency for whom they actually worked, were bound to a common cause. Most lived in government housing, their children attended the same schools, and even the children were treated like military personnel inasmuch as we were all issued dog tags and we participated in the same, now somewhat humorous, crouch-under-your desk atomic attack drills. In a way, the place was a great equalizer of people and contributed to why I continue to promote and employ an inverted, upside-down organizational chart, where those who have the most direct contact with prospects, customers, the market, and the work are the ones at the top. *They are our most important employees and the ones to whom we must listen very intently.*

But a lot of how Oak Ridge contributed to my unique formative years also has to do with the reality that the whole city, like the product it was created to produce, was a grand experiment. The scientists of Oak Ridge were literally working with materials in ways no one had before. That meant some of the greatest minds of the generation lived there. It also meant that a lot of how they lived was experimental as well. This was definitely true of our schools. The result was an educational system that was so far advanced that we were exposed to teaching methods and approaches that were not common. For example, starting about a quarter of the way through our second grade year, some of us who were excelling in our studies were sent *back* to the first grade classes for part of the day to serve as teacher aides of a sort, where we helped the younger kids learn. I assume that the concept was something I continue to adopt with employees today: In order to truly learn something, you need to prove that you can teach it to someone else. There is no room for winging it when you are trying to teach someone, and any shortcomings in your own knowledge become glaringly apparent. Teaching someone else forces you to learn and communicate in entirely new ways. You begin to focus on learning and teaching in the same sphere. If I know how to do something, but I can't teach someone else how to do it, then I have become the bottleneck for growth, and we are stymied. I need to be able to demonstrate and explain a new concept, and new method, a new process in a way that can be easily understood, digested, and effectively employed by the recipient of the information.

Classes in Oak Ridge were unusual and experimental in other ways too. In third grade, everyone was required to begin studying a foreign language, French. There is nothing more basic than the languages we speak. You can't learn anything unless you have access to it, and language is an access portal. To encounter something as comprehensive and elemental as a new language so early in life made learning lots of other new things easier. The point wasn't so much about gaining fluency, although that could come with time and con-sistency over the years, but about exposure and opening new parts of the brain. These kinds of approaches extended our view of what was possible. They enlightened us to the possibility of considering new—even revolutionary—ideas and approaches and exposed us to experiences and viewpoints different from our own.

There was another element to a place like Oak Ridge and the nature of those who lived there, something that also came out of the assumption that it would be a temporary place. When you lived in virtually identical houses and went to the same school whether your parents were nuclear physicists or truck drivers, there was no comparing academic abilities or family bank accounts; you all learned the same curriculum in the same way, and you were doing so in a system where people believed in excellence and the value of learning. As I got to know some of the parents of my friends and people with whom my dad worked, I began to understand two vital truths. First, all of those adults, including those who were, literally, rocket scientists, were just humans; they could be funny or stern or have interesting hobbies or share things I appreciated, like going fishing or camping, or things I'd never encountered before, like opera or foods that were not staples in our house. Second, everyone arrived at Oak Ridge along different paths, from different places around the world or the country and from different upbringings. I think this aspect of living in Oak Ridge helped formulate the second truth I discovered, which became the foundational first mantra I shared earlier: The biggest difference between people who do and people who don't is that people who do simply believe they can. What's behind that belief is not simply God-given talent. It's not IQ. It's not the size of their bank account. It's not the number of educational degrees behind their name or their family pedigree. They just have something in them—a conviction— that compels them to believe and say, "I can do that." Even when they can't do it, even when they fail, they possess some ego strength—ego strength, not ego, for the difference is vast—that makes them believe, "I can figure out how to fix what made that fail."

I would identify at least one more aspect of my childhood that has helped define me and make me less afraid of being different or failing. While we moved on from Oak Ridge to Memphis when I was about to turn eight years old, my roots, and my accent, were decidedly indigenous to East Tennessee. True to my origins, I not only have a strong southern accent but a distinctive East Tennessee accent. People tend to react in different ways to southern accents, depending on the nature of their own experience and where they are from. Some find southern accents charming, which allows you to get away with a lot. Some associate southern accents with low intelligence, which is simply a case of ignorance, and I've already established the distinction between ignorance and stupidity. Since I grew up in the South, for me, it's just how people talk.

But a lot of the opportunities I seized in the early stages of my career took me to the Rust Belt in the Upper Midwest and to the northeastern United States and eventually to a multiyear assignment in Europe. I had already encountered some ridicule about my accent back in junior high (called middle school now) when our family moved from Memphis to Greenwood, South Carolina, for a brief period of time, and I was reminded once again how my accent could be seen either as an asset or as a liability. I remember once I was working with a client in Massachusetts who said to his colleagues and associates on meeting me, "People are going to hear Toby and they're going to take advantage of him. We have to take care of him." The result of them "taking care" of this poor old southern boy made me a lot of money! Exercising the long antennas to which I referred earlier, I learned to modulate my accent a bit to fit the audience and maximize effectiveness, especially when executing formal speaking engagements. However, when doing so, I was always cognizant of remaining true to who I really am, including those foundational elements of my background that come through in my voice. Something as simple but as integral to who we are as the essence of our voice is a reminder of another critical mantra for excellence: Turn what most people would consider a liability, whether in business or in life, into an asset. Some people might say doing so is simply having a positive attitude. But I think it's more than that because you really have to think through how you are going to leverage any so-called liability for a competitive advantage, whether that is creating a competitive edge in the markets you serve or elevating and expanding the positive influence you have on the people around you.

When we hold this attitude of leveraging liabilities into assets, we extend what Ken Blanchard wrote in *The One Minute Manager* when he expressed that "everyone is a potential winner. Some people are disguised as losers. Don't let their appearance fool you." I believe that. Everyone has something to offer. Making the most of who we are awakens each of us to the idea that we can help illuminate and extend that same possibility to everyone around us. Finding the positive traits in others and encouraging them to put those talents to work for the enterprise is a central part of leadership. I think it's a central part of life as well. God doesn't call us to judge people; he calls us to love them. That doesn't mean you don't correct people when they have made an error or that you're not tough on them when it's appropriate, but let's concentrate on finding the good in those around us. Let's accentuate their strengths. As Marcus Buckingham proposed in his book, *First, Break All the Rules*, let's figure out what's already in people and draw it out of them.

Finding the good in others has been a central theme of my leadership approach for a long, long time. I attribute any success that I have experienced to having learned to make the most of what I have and trying to help others do the same. I have worked in manufacturing, professional service, and technology companies. Over the years, I crystallized my own approach to leading people and growing companies, and since 2006, I have been fortunate to hold the top spot—president, partner, CEO—of apparel, technology, consulting, and marketing companies that have grown rapidly and achieved unprecedented levels of revenue and profitability. I don't take that for granted, and I didn't do it alone.

> Finding the positive traits in others and encouraging them to put those talents to work for the enterprise is a central part of leadership.

I've experienced some degree of success by never forgetting where I come from or the lessons I learned along the way. That in turn has created something else that I view as essential to leadership—the desire to give back. Winston Churchill wisely said, "We make a living by what we get. We make a life by what we give." I've tried to do so when opportunities have been presented to me that play to my strengths and that can truly move the needle relative to extending a better quality of life and economic prosperity to a broader expanse of our community, state, and world. Pursuing professional opportunities, I moved to Asheville, North Carolina, in 1982; to Maastricht, Netherlands, in 1995; took a position with a company headquartered just north of Los Angeles in 1998; and moved to Austin, Texas, in 2002. I have had the privilege of working in forty-five of the fifty states and across much of Europe and Asia. I returned to Greenville, South Carolina (where I first moved in 1978), at the end of 2004, and I have been here since then. Many of the experiences of my life as a follower and as a leader have been shared with organizations local to Greenville and the surrounding upstate area. From its inception in 2010, I cochaired, with Craig Brown, Accelerate!, the Greenville Chamber's economic development initiative. Craig, the owner of the local minor league baseball team, and I served together in these roles for eleven years until we resigned in 2020 to devote our collective efforts to reinvigorating the entrepreneurial community in Upstate South Carolina. I served on the board of directors of the Greenville Chamber for nine years and filled the role of vice chair of economic competitiveness on the chamber's strategic cabinet for seven years. I have been fortunate to have won the Greenville Chamber's Chairman's Award twice, and in 2020, I was honored with the Buck Mickel Award, the Greenville Chamber's most prestigious award for business leadership. I served on the board of

> I attribute any success that I have experienced to having learned to make the most of what I have and trying to help others do the same.

Clemson's Spiro Institute for Entrepreneurship and Innovation. I filled the role of chair of the advisory board for the first four years of the Greenville Chamber's Minority Business Accelerator and for the next three years served as its instructor. I was a regular podium fixture at Clemson's Center for Corporate Learning's Leadership Symposium and for the same organization's miniMBA program. I have, for the past four years, served as the author and instructor for their Narrative Leadership course.

I share these activities and accomplishments not because I in any way think I'm special, important, or influential. That is not the point at all. *The only reason that I even mention any of these appointments, awards, or achievements is to encourage you to make a difference—because you can.* None of these opportunities would have ever entered my life if I hadn't said yes to them, even when I wasn't certain that I was qualified. I would never have had the opportunity to meet the extraordinary people I encountered or engage with the organizations that invited me to participate if I gave into fear or if I believed that the limits of any natural abilities I possessed would limit my effectiveness. I still maintain the same attitude I had as a kid who wasn't going to let a hole in his heart hold him back or serve as an excuse for failure.

MANTRAS FOR EXCELLENCE:

O   Don't defend it; deal with it.

O   "It's my fault. Blame me."

O   Never allow another person's failure to be an excuse for your own.

O   To develop new leaders, you have to be willing to tolerate a reasonable degree of failure.

Chapter 3

IT'S EITHER RESULTS
OR EXCUSES

There's an old saying: it's either results or excuses. The standard is the standard. If you fail, as an authentic leader, you have to own it. Then you had better figure out how to do it better next time. Rule one on finding a solution: I have to find a way to win—legally, morally, and ethically—regardless of the rules imposed on me by the marketplace, the competition, my customers, or our personnel within the bounds of our organization. That remains true even if one of the rules is that I have to fight with one hand tied behind my back. To help the leaders of organizations learn how to make wise decisions and determine when they can and cannot make unilateral decisions, I crafted a simple decision-making model. The third tenet in the model puts some guardrails around the types of decisions that can be made unilaterally. Those limits are what I call the six Cs: A leader is free to make any decision within their span of control, body of knowledge, or area of expertise, as long as the decision doesn't unnecessarily put our *company*, our *culture*, an important *customer*, a significant *contract*, your *character*, or your *confidence* at risk.

When I was president of Acumen IT, I had a young IT engineer who, while experimenting with an automated messaging feature, changed a piece of code and inadvertently sent an incorrect message to a few hundred of our customers. I had seen the message when it came through after hours. The next morning, the employee walked in my office and said, "Man, I screwed up last night." Then he told me what he'd done. He had already commissioned all of our engineers to begin alerting our customers about the error. Even though he was obviously distressed, he had the presence of mind to recall the lessons we had built into our corporate culture about personal and professional accountability, and he stopped in the middle of a sentence and said, "Oh, before I forget. This is my fault. I was the person who caused this to happen."

> ## THE SIX Cs:
>
> Never make a unilateral decision that is of such a magnitude that, were you to be wrong, it would irreparably or catastrophically damage:
>
> - Our company
> - Our culture
> - An important customer
> - A significant contract
> - Your character
> - Your confidence

Man, what a victory for a developing leader and for our organization! I was thrilled to hear him take ownership of his decision and its aftermath. So I asked him, "How bad is it? Did your decision and the consequences destroy one of the six Cs?"

"I don't think so. We are working on the problem, and beyond some personal embarrassment, I think it's recoverable."

I said, "Fine. What'd you learn?"

He replied, "I learned I'm never doing that again!"

"Well," I said, "I guess we're one step closer to getting it right. Now get outta my office!"

Don't defend it; deal with it. Real leaders are vulnerable. They readily admit—and they mean it—when they are wrong. Too often we are hypocritical and hold people to high standards but then won't hold ourselves to the same standards. Leaders say, *and mean it*, as that young man did, "It's my fault. Blame me." To be able to do so is the development of ego strength, the ability to encounter failure, to own it, and to get off the ground, dust yourself off, and keep going. To unfailingly hold on to and live up to your respect for the truth by admitting fault and fallibility when the easy out would be to blame your failure on someone else, on a failed process, or on a faulty procedure. When there is something that needs repair in the latter two—processes or procedures— authentic leaders take the blame first and then do whatever is necessary to fix the problem so that it doesn't happen again. Sometimes the problem is me. And I have to fix it. Within the framework of the six Cs and the bounds of legality and ethics, it's my job to be resourceful, to be creative, and *to find a way to win*. One of my mantras is never allow another person's failure to be an excuse for your own. Anytime you offer an excuse, you've become self-limiting, and you are stifling your own professional development. During my career, I've never gotten better at anything by behaving like a card-

> Real leaders are vulnerable. They readily admit— and they mean it—when they are wrong.

carrying member of the Mutual Admiration Society, a fictitious name given to that very real elite club of company cronies who constantly pat each other on the back and tell each other how good they are. Don't buy into that narrative. Don't build a padded story line for yourself just because it protects you. Doing so only puts you in a cocoon so that you don't have to deal with shortcomings in your life. You will never get any better if you do that.

We must hold ourselves to high standards while knowing all along that we are never going to be perfect. I have to *readily* admit when I'm wrong. Because the truth is that no one is perfect and we're never going to be. Tripping into the occasional pothole is part of life. That's so true that my wife won't let me use the word *mistake* when I do something wrong. Instead, she makes me say, "I made a bad choice." She's right. We're all going to make some bad choices. The question is, Will we own our choices? Will we stand up and take responsibility? Will we do what it takes to not make the same bad choice again? Anything less is just an excuse.

The same is true about casting blame. That's really just another brand of excuse. How many times have you heard people in your organization say, "We would have made that sale...hit that budget number...met the deadline...except you-know-who didn't do their part." What's the old saying? "If ifs and buts were candy and nuts, my wouldn't Christmas be all year long!" My philosophy is this: we need to need to eliminate the words *if* and *but* from our vocabularies, because as long as we have a reason or an excuse for underperformance, we will never improve to the degree necessary to achieve our ultimate potential.

Our job as leaders is to help others learn to accept their responsibilities within their sphere of influence and help them grow. That starts by never passing judgment on people as to their present position in life or in business. It's way more important to understand how to help a person get pointed in the right direction than to be overly concerned about their current station in life. Life is much more about where you're headed than it is about where you are. If we can be a positive influence in people's lives by helping them learn to accept responsibility and develop a commitment and desire to produce results, sometimes we can help them turn a few degrees and see something they don't see. That's the same thing I want people to do for me when I'm facing a tough decision or trying to navigate our way out of a problem. To develop new leaders, you have to be willing to tolerate a reasonable degree of failure.

> Our job as leaders is to help others learn to accept their responsibilities within their sphere of influence and help them grow.

We can always find reasons for failure or poor performance. Don't use them. In order to avoid excuses, you have to build a culture that balances empowerment and accountability. Empowerment without accountability is anarchy or chaos. But accountability without bestowing true empowerment or authority fosters paralysis. Empowerment and accountability go hand in hand. One without the other causes more problems than it solves.

Building a climate or culture that supports empowerment requires that we get on the same page as an organization. First, you must build a core ideology for yourself, one consisting of four elements:

- Purpose: "Why do I exist?"
- Vision: "What do I want to become?"
- Mission: "What do I want to achieve?"
- Values: "What character traits do I want to embody?"

Then the organization, working together, needs to build a core ideology that all agree upon and act upon every day, working in a unified, coordinated manner:

- Purpose: "Why do we exist?"

- Vision: "What do we want to become?"

- Mission: "What do we want to achieve?"

- Values: "What character traits do we want to embody?"

Organizational values include empowering individuals with the ability to make decisions and shepherd projects, which in turn creates an acceptance of accountability that can be infused into the entire organization. They become the values by which we live collectively because we believe in them individually and we hold ourselves to high standards. In order for companies to meet the same high standards, the leaders and all team members hold one another accountable. Accountability drives commitment, which in turn fosters the motivation to innovate. The companies that have the mental and physical agility required to admit failure and change direction are the ones that gain competitive advantage because they figure out a better way to do something. Again, this mentality must be intrinsic. I don't want a customer or my competition to illuminate our weaknesses; I need to beat them to the punch. It is from this kind of regular and rigorous introspection and mental agility that helped me formulate an approach to fixing problems and improving processes that

THE FOUR As MODEL:

- Adopt
- Adapt
- Apply
- Adjust

I call the four As model: adopt, adapt, apply, and adjust. This approach is key to achieving and sustaining a competitive edge, as it leverages external knowledge and resources to accelerate the development and deployment of innovative, effective solutions.

The root of the model suggests that the fastest way to success is to identify and adopt an approach that is already working for another person or firm and adapt it for our own use. As people and as organizations, we don't have to invent or create from whole cloth everything that we use. Find something that works in a similar situation, adopt it as your starting point, and keep tweaking it until it works better—until it is optimized. You listen to other people; you study history; you search Google and YouTube; you learn from other companies, other thinkers, other colleagues; and you *adopt* an existing approach that shows promise. You *adapt* it to fit your particular situation, you *apply* it by putting the process or approach into service, and then, based on measurable results, you *adjust* as needed to optimize performance and results. It's an approach that can and will work for any size and type of organization or project.

When you put the four As model to work in a consistent manner, there's a unique shift in an organization's leadership culture. When everyone is on the same page relative to identifying, deploying, and optimizing solutions, decision-making responsibility can be more broadly distributed across the organization. While it is true that you can delegate authority but not responsibility, the pressure to make the best decisions no longer resides only in the corner office. You'll find yourself regularly saying, "Let's do it your way." That will become one of the most powerful and impactful five-word phrases you'll ever utter, and exploring why is where we'll go next.

MANTRAS FOR EXCELLENCE:

O The distance between informed and ignorant is really short. Make sure you don't travel too far.

O Ignorance is nothing more than not knowing.

O The biggest difference between people who do and people who don't is that people who do simply believe they can.

O Every individual's level of expectation and understanding is directly related to their prior degree of exposure.

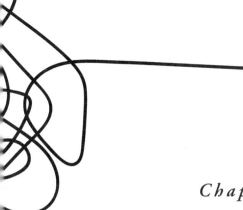

Chapter 4

PEOPLE WHO DO SIMPLY
BELIEVE THEY CAN

If you have gotten this far in the book, you probably recall me imploring you in an earlier chapter to relish the state of ignorance. You might read this statement and think I am crazy. Why would anyone want to be ignorant? The distance between informed and ignorant is really short. Make sure you don't travel too far. I have to go all the way back to my high school chemistry class—it and some other courses that scared me badly enough in college that I went looking for a major that kept me as far away from such subjects as possible, which landed me in finance—but I am mindful that in chemistry, *state* refers to the condition of a system at a given time. A state is temporary. As I learned early in my life, ignorance is nothing more than the state of not knowing. The cure for any state of ignorance starts with a simple commitment to learn new things. We train ourselves not to be embarrassed but instead to relish the state of ignorance because it means we have the opportunity to rectify it. We can choose to learn anything we want.

I'm a naturally curious person. I'm fascinated by learning new facts and understanding how and why things work. Early in my sales career, I would walk into a textile plant or a manufacturing facility and want to know everything about the processes, from how materials arrived at the facility, to how the equipment worked, to how the product was assembled or manufactured, to how it got to its final destination and was put in use by the customer. That natural intellectual curiosity was awakened in me at an early age and certainly was furthered by the unique school environment of my early life and by watching my dad, who was an engineer.

> The cure for any state of ignorance starts with a simple commitment to learn new things.

Sometimes my exposure to and immediate fascination with something turned into more than a passing interest. For example, when I was fourteen or fifteen, probably because I paid attention to my dad, I decided to try my hand at repairing fishing rods. That's where the roots reside for one of the side jobs I still worked when I started my first real-life, postcollege employment. Like my dad, I love to fish. As embarrassing as it is to admit, I have 105 fishing rods in my garage, and I don't even fish that much anymore. Dad had a fly-tying vise, but rather than tie flies, he used it to make "hatticalls," the distinctly southern term for lead-headed jigs that you use to catch crappie. He would use old tire weights, melt them down in a mold he had, and then take dyed polar bear hair and tie it around the lead head and hook using nylon thread. He would complete the process by sealing the threads with a waterproofing sealer made at the time by Testors that was called "airplane dope." The airplane dope sealed the thread to the lead head and strengthened the knot that tied off the thread so that it wouldn't loosen in the water.

It was watching Pop that gave me an idea. If you fish enough, it's inevitable that you are going to snap off a line guide or break a rod. While we live in an age where most people would throw away a rod and replace it or learn to live with a missing guide, I didn't grow up around such people. Those who I knew learned how to do things for themselves and were quick to employ practical solutions. So I decided to build a wooden contraption (a rod-making jig) that would support a fishing rod. I ordered from an industrial supply house a small 25-rpm motor, salvaged a rheostatic pedal from one of my mom's sewing machines, and wired the pedal to the motor so that it would allow me to use my foot to control the speed of a rod turning in the jig. To hold the butt of the rod, I bought rubber crutch tips of various sizes into which I inserted a machine screw (bolt) that I could screw into a threaded chuck that attached to the shaft of the 25-rpm motor. It wasn't glamourous, but it worked, which made me wonder if I couldn't build my own rods from scratch. I bought a book on rod making and studied some articles in magazines. I ordered some more motors and made two more rod-making jigs and began ordering blanks and rod parts from a company in Texas. I learned how to improve the process with each rod I built. Before long, I began creating unique and visually attractive thread patterns to decorate the butt end of the rods and wrap the guides onto the rods. I usually applied an elaborate diamond pattern using multiple colors of threads that I wrapped onto the butt of the rod that was then coated in a couple of layers of epoxy. Eventually I was selling rods across the country, and to further personalize each customer's rod, I used dry transfer script lettering to put the customer's name on the finished rod, instinctively understanding that most people take pride in owning something that is truly one of a kind. Now I look at the 105 rods in my garage and realize that, as a teenager, *no one told me I couldn't* build fishing rods. I simply followed my curiosity. I learned about something that fascinated me. It's a lesson I hold on to. There is real joy in learning, and I try to never go to bed without having learned something new that day.

As adults, particularly as leaders, in order to apply the remedy for ignorance and learn something new, you have to first face down fear. Fear comes in a lot of forms, and whether we admit it or not, most of us fear looking stupid in front of others. One of the realities is that the more frequently you overcome fear, take risks, and open yourself to new experiences, the more confident you grow. It's not always easy, but it is almost always worth it in the end.

Early in my career, while I was working for Jobscope, John Hoffman, the CEO of a company called Right Source, called me out of the blue and said, "You don't know who I am, but I've been scouting you for a while." John had been with IBM for a portion of his career and still had contacts there and was aware of my performance at IBM a few years earlier. "I'm wondering if you might be the right person to help me grow this new company I started." Right Source produced executive technology seminars for IBM and other large technology companies as a means to market new products. I viewed myself as a salesperson, and I really knew very little about marketing. It just didn't seem like a great fit for my skills and experience, so I thanked him for his interest and told John that I was going to stay where I was. Something about John's interest, however, stuck in my mind, and two or three years later, when I was thinking about moving from Jobscope, I gave John a call. He told me he was in Connecticut but genuinely wanted to talk to me, so he asked me to clear time for lunch the next day because he was going to fly down to South Carolina that night.

I soon learned that John had tremendous instincts for understanding people, and somehow he had figured out, without ever meeting me in person, that I had a real affinity for new challenges and opportunities. By the end of lunch the next day, he had convinced me to come to Right Source, even though the role that I was going to fill was a little murky at that point. Unbeknownst to me, John had a desire to expand Right Source into Europe, and he was banking on his instincts that once I got oriented to the business, I was the right person to establish a Right Source beachhead in Europe. Less than three months after my arrival, John let the cat out of the bag. What John didn't know was this: I had only been outside the United States for a few days during my entire life. While I was working at Jobscope, we recruited a software dealer in Montreal, Canada, and I had taken a few trips there to help them with their sales efforts. But John had an uncanny knack for reading people, and he knew that the scale of the challenge and a grand new adventure would be very intriguing to me.

Within weeks, Susan and I took a reconnaissance trip to the Netherlands. We flew into Amsterdam and spent a few days there with some local representatives who squired us around and showed us places where we could live and facilities that would be suitable to house Right Source Europe. I won't lie. I found the city intimidating, not just for its size and pace of life but for the obvious reasons when finding myself in a foreign country where I didn't speak the language, didn't know my way around, and wasn't familiar with the culture. I didn't even recognize much of the food that we ate. Yet the novelty of a grand new undertaking was simultaneously exciting. We felt adventurous. After a couple of days in Amsterdam, we visited Maastricht, a charming medieval city in the south of Holland near the Belgian and German borders, and it felt like a culturally vibrant place with some southern (Southern Netherlands!) charm and familiarity, a place we thought could serve as a home base while exploring a new career and a new place. We made the decision to establish Right Source Europe, and once we returned for good in July 1995, our small team of three expatriate Americans buckled down and began learning the place, the people, and the business, intent on figuring out our company and the new country and culture in which we now found ourselves.

The job held as many unfamiliar lessons as the Dutch language. Our presence in Europe was to open with a multicity tour promoting the IBM AS/400 computer. The marketing model we were importing from the United States staged technology seminars in major metropolitan cities, inviting all the top-level executives from the region's biggest companies. We would host them at grand hotels or other high-end, upscale venues and cater in excellent meals—breakfast before morning seminars or lunch before seminars that were scheduled for the afternoon. The seminar was comprised of a three-hour presentation and demonstration of some of IBM's latest technology. Before we had even gotten started, however, our team went to Paris to get our marching orders and tour plan from the IBM AS/400 executive there with whom we had worked in the States but who was now in Paris to initiate a similar program for Europe. I knew something was amiss the minute I walked in the IBM EMEA office in Paris and saw Mr. Duncan. Unbelievably, the words that came out of his mouth went something like this: "Toby, I don't know how to tell you this. Our priorities have changed. We've reallocated the funding that we had designated for the European AS/400 technology tour. It's not going to happen." That project was intended to generate the seed money that we needed to firmly establish Right Source and justify our European operation. There was talk among us on the train ride back to Maastricht that we needed to hop on a plane, return to the States, and forget this pipe dream. But collectively, we determined that we would figure it out. First, we would have to find someone to lead the seminars. We identified and connected with an IBM AS/400 specialist in Hamburg, Germany, Frank Buechler. When we told Frank about the pan-European AS/400 tour that had been canceled, not only did Frank express an eagerness to help us, he also shared with us that he had been trying to get IBM Deutschland to plan and execute a similar AS/400 promotional tour in Germany. With Frank's help, we met with IBM executives in Stuttgart and landed a six-city Germany tour that went so well that we parlayed its success into a larger European tour for other IBM technologies.

Nearly every day of that second, more-expansive tour produced something unexpected. Not only were we hopping from one country and one culture to another, but we were met with circumstances that constantly demanded that we be flexible in our problem-solving abilities. In Milan, for instance, not only were we shocked to arrive and find that our host hotel was building a sizable, elaborate temporary venue fit for a rock concert for our event, but we opened our equipment cases only to find all of our ThinkPads (i.e., notebook computers) missing. Whatever the circumstances of their disappearance—thieves, a problem at customs, poor fate—they were gone, and we had a show to put on within eighteen hours. The ThinkPads were housed in portable cases that also contained IBM servers and allowed us to assemble an entire computer network onstage. Without the ThinkPads, we were sunk. We had a young engineer with us, Paul Anderson, who said that if he used one of the team member's personal laptops, he thought he could download the software and presentation materials we required and that were housed on our servers/computers in America. However, this was 1995, the age of dial-up internet access. "It might take me all night," Paul said, "but I think I can do it." He succeeded in rebuilding the entire network, and the show went off with no one any the wiser.

The Milan story demonstrates a number of traits critical to business success—teamwork, flexibility in problem-solving, perseverance—and it absolutely is instructive in the four As model. But underlying all those traits is a willingness to simply get things done, to find a way. Working in countries to which most of us had never traveled before, navigating unfamiliar languages and cultures, and immersing ourselves daily in places and among people who were entirely new made us turn to our own resolve to find ways to succeed. While working abroad, like traveling internationally for pleasure, is truly invigorating and eye-opening, it is demanding. The most ordinary transactions become complicated when you don't share a common language or when you encounter an obstacle with which you have absolutely zero prior experience or understanding as to how to address, even if that's just getting from point A to point C via public transport. People tend to either avoid such environments or, knowing the joy and wonder that can be experienced when they embrace the unfamiliar, they adopt a personal belief that they can accomplish the mission whether miniscule in scope or grandiose. It's one of those funny ironies in life, for as kids, most of us wanted to join in rather than shy away in fear; as teens, we likely thought we were invincible and the surest way to get us to do something was to tell us we couldn't; yet as adults, we spend a lot of time trying to blend in and not be found out when we don't know something. On the other hand, leaders not only have an insatiable need to learn things, but the best of them also create practical and innovative ways to move people and businesses in entirely new directions, even when it is uncomfortable. Every individual's level of understanding and expectation is directly related to their prior degree of exposure.

On our European tours with Right Source, the more we presented, the more in demand we became. We were soon contracted to produce seminars in countries that were formerly behind the Iron Curtain, in the former Czech Republic, Hungary, and Russia. From there we went to the Middle East, including a program in Tel Aviv. Every day offered new fascinations and new challenges. Sometimes we encountered moments that were downright scary, like dealing with authoritarian government bureaucrats or corruption among criminal entities that ran roughshod through the unions that hauled our equipment. I sent a young American who had moved with us to Europe to help staff one of our events in Tel Aviv. One evening the following week, he was sitting in our family room in Maastricht after completing a long day at work. On the evening news, a story was being covered about a suicide bomber who had attacked a Tel Aviv bus, destroying the bus and killing a number of passengers and bystanders. My young colleague grew quiet, and when I asked him what was up, he said, "I was standing on that exact street corner one week ago today."

> Leaders not only have an insatiable need to learn things, but the best of them also create practical and innovative ways to move people and businesses in entirely new directions, even when it is uncomfortable.

The world that had once seemed abstract and far away had become immediate and personal. Novel experiences that had once seemed intimidating jump-started something in me. The more and more exposed I was to new ideas and new adventures, the more an insatiable drive grew. My vision of travel became one where I didn't really want to visit the places I'd seen before. I had been there, done that. I craved new and interesting places where I might see something I had never seen before and where I could meet people from all walks of life. That craving carried forward into my professional life. I sought new ventures, welcomed new challenges, and explored other industries. What had started as a fear that I couldn't do marketing was transformed over time to a quiet confidence that my leadership skills could be transferred and effectively employed in executive roles within industry sectors with which I was largely unfamiliar, including apparel and consulting, and even to a CEO role for an ad agency.

What I had learned was that the biggest difference between people who do and people who don't is not their IQ, family name, educational degrees, or level of wealth. The biggest difference is that people who do simply believe they can. There is something in them that drives them to believe and say, "I'm going to find a way." People who don't change their state of ignorance many times are stymied because they are frozen in place by insecurity. It's human nature to not want to be embarrassed, so many of us refuse to put ourselves in environments where we might be forced to reveal our ignorance or lack of experience. Instead of feeling insecure, when in an unfamiliar environment, learn to inject yourself fully into it so that you can learn more. Remember the mantra I shared earlier: Everyone's level of expectation and understanding is directly related to their prior degree of exposure. The more you allow yourself to be exposed to new things, even if you feel stupid, even if you're ignorant, the more you broaden and deepen your body of knowledge and grow your personal and professional toolkit. We are all ignorant about things we have never encountered or experienced. It's a global common denominator. But the more you show others that you're not afraid to try new things, tackle new challenges, admit when you don't know, and do something to change that state, the more of an authentic, inspiring leader you will become.

MANTRAS FOR EXCELLENCE:

O   Most individuals still make decisions emotionally and support them rationally.

O   Your organizational chart might say otherwise, but your real manager is you—no one else.

O   Most people can do twice as much as they are currently doing—qualitatively and quantitatively.

O   "Excellence is not an act; it's a habit." —Carl Sobocinski

O   Freedom isn't being able to do anything you want to do; freedom is having the power to do what you know you ought to do.

O   Many times the things we want to do the least are the things we ought to do the most.

O   "Great performers set goals and achieve results. Great leaders set goals and achieve results through others." —Dr. David Mutchler and Linda Martin

O   "If you think you're leading, but no one is following, then you are only taking a walk." —John Maxwell

O   "A life is not important except in the impact it has on others' lives." —Jackie Robinson

O   All meaningful and lasting change starts first on the inside and works its way out.

Chapter 5

THE TEST OF PERSONAL AND PROFESSIONAL MATURITY

Overcoming fear and becoming a doer take a certain amount of maturity. How many people have failed not because they truly failed but because they never tried? Most individuals still make decisions emotionally and support them rationally. Overcoming fear is only a first step. Once you are determined to overcome fear and take action to remedy your ignorance, it takes discipline to be a self-directed learner and a self-motivated doer. In order to create opportunities for intentional exposure to new things and new ideas, you must develop intrinsic motivation. Applying what you learn to situations with which you are not intimately familiar and in which you will certainly experience false steps and dead ends takes greater discipline still. Successful people

> Once you are determined to overcome fear and take action to remedy your ignorance, it takes discipline to be a self-directed learner and a self-motivated doer.

understand the need to be self-managed. Your organizational chart might say otherwise, but your real manager is you—no one else. Successful people don't need others to push them; they supply that force for themselves.

Children, and all parents know this, have to be instructed to take nearly any action *that is good for them:* "Brush your teeth." "Go to bed." "Eat your vegetables." Somewhere along the way, most of us eventually learn how to intrinsically manage our lives; we no longer need to be told to perform the basics of living. Yet, incredulously, we are all too familiar with employees who, for whatever reason, never develop an appropriate level of professional initiative and still need to be told what to do, no matter their degree of experience. If you regularly encounter such employees within your span of control or responsibility, you need to ask yourself if you are cultivating a culture that fosters dependence instead of self-development and taking calculated risks while rewarding excellent failures. At a minimum, you may have a problem in your hiring process, or worse, *you* may be the problem. In the enterprises I have helped lead, one of the essential requirements is that we hire self-starters. Someone once said, "If you want something done, ask the busiest person you know." With every hire, I am searching for employees who have an innate desire to punch above their fighting weight by taking on responsibilities that demand skills and expertise that are just beyond their current level of expertise and experience. It takes maturity, initiative, and discipline to be that sort of employee. We need team members who don't wait for a boss to tell them to take action but who actively scan the horizon looking for what needs done. They are disciplined enough to ask the question that serves as the motto this year at Cargo, the marketing solutions company I presently lead: "What's most important *right now?*" A lack of discipline or intrinsic motivation to ask and answer this question *every day* is a sign of immaturity or professional inertia.

My experience in working with, managing, and leading team members for more than four decades is that most people can do twice as much as they are currently doing—qualitatively and quantitatively. There are three reasons why they don't. Rather than learning to relish the state of ignorance, they claim their lack of knowledge as an excuse. "No one ever told me that" and "No one showed me how to do that" are two of the most common explanations offered in the workplace. There are no excuses lamer than these. Living in the Information Age, "not knowing" can almost always easily be remedied, for the answers are many times no further away than posing a question to a search engine or making an inquiry on Google or YouTube. Ninety-five percent of everything we want to know or need to do has probably already been mastered, and recorded, by someone else. Rather than invest time, money, and effort to invent solutions out of whole cloth, why not research what has already been done and use that as your starting point? We all have to remind ourselves to search for answers in the public domain first, as so many times today, the information we are seeking is right at our fingertips—literally.

That leaves us with the second reason why people are not more productive: They won't push themselves. However you wish to label it—persistence, grit, discipline, determination—without such a personality trait, you are rarely going to win. I know this firsthand. I spent too many years just getting by. I was fortunate to have been born with a reasonable level of intelligence. I could read at three years old. By age five, I could recognize any make of car or truck, even at night, just by the type of headlights the vehicle had. School came easily. I received straight As until the seventh grade, when I started slacking off. Even then, I always liked learning, but I didn't consistently apply myself. I learned to goof off. By high school, I typically gave minimal effort, and I still managed to graduate thirty-fifth in a class of 713. We had moved from South Carolina to North Carolina at the beginning of my eleventh grade year. I was a good enough student to be a finalist for a Morehead Scholarship at the University of North Carolina, which offered room and board, tuition, books, and even a small amount of monthly spending money. I made it through the school interview and county and district interviews. The rumor was that if you made it to the last step, an interview on campus in Chapel Hill, you were a lock. It turned out that I wasn't a lock. I was so out of step with the application process, mostly out of pure laziness (and not paying attention to readily available information), that I didn't even know that UNC was a liberal arts school, yet on my application I had declared that I was going to major in mechanical engineering. You can guess what the first question from the Chapel Hill interviewers was.

I was still offered a tuition-only scholarship to UNC, but I chose to return to South Carolina and go to Clemson instead. I excelled there for my first year, recording a 3.7 grade point average. But bad habits crept in. By my sophomore year, I began to sleep in and miss class, and my GPA started to decline. I put more effort into selling stereo equipment than I put into coursework. I failed to graduate with honors because I didn't give my best effort, and I resorted to getting by on raw intelligence. That pattern persisted as I entered the workforce. My first job was in Raleigh, North Carolina, designing and selling business forms, and not only did I find the work boring, but the entire business forms industry was hurtling toward obsolescence due to the advent of computer and printing technology. This was an eventuality that was glaringly obvious, but I was oblivious to this development because I didn't invest the time and effort to stay abreast of technology trends, again failing to pay attention to what should have been obvious (even if it wasn't to my employers).

Throughout high school, I worked summers and Christmas breaks in one of Guilford Mills's textile plants in Greensboro, North Carolina. My dad was vice president of engineering at Guilford, and he made sure that I had "special" working hours at the mill. My dad usually worked from 8:30 a.m. to 5:30 p.m., but my job was on first shift, which ran from 7:00 a.m. to 3:00 p.m. Our family had only two vehicles, so my dad decided that he would go in at seven each day so that I could ride to work with him and be on time for the start time of my shift. However, he worked out an arrangement with the plant manager that would allow me to work until 5:30 p.m. Monday through Friday so that I wasn't sitting around for two and a half hours waiting for him to take me home at five thirty. So instead of an eight-hour shift, I worked a ten-and-a-half-hour shift each day. The icing on the cake was that once I graduated from doffing cloth to unloading warp beams—giant spools of yarn—from tractor trailers with a forklift, I also worked every Saturday morning from 8:00 a.m. to 12:00 p.m. because that was when the dock workers unloaded the trailers and restocked the yarn inventory. So my normal workweek was fifty-six and a half hours. I really didn't mind, because that meant I got paid overtime for sixteen and a half hours, but the real benefit was that I became a certified forklift (towmotor) driver, which meant I got to drive a forklift most of the day, which was a heck of a lot better than pushing a floor dolly around the mill and doffing cloth all day.

After I had graduated college and taken my first job selling business forms in Raleigh, North Carolina, Dad called me one day and told me that Vann Williford, the co-owner of Vesco, the largest Toyota forklift dealer in the country, was looking for a South Carolina salesperson. I jumped at this chance, thinking, "I know something about forklifts and about southern industries, and this will take me back to South Carolina and closer to Clemson, where I attended college." I was twenty-two years old, and while I might have had natural instincts for selling, as I had been reasonably successful selling stereo equipment and fishing rods, I was green and naive. Remember, this was 1978. It never occurred to me that I was signing on to sell a high-quality but relatively new Japanese product into textile plants and other industrial organizations where the parking lots were filled with American-made pickup trucks and muscle cars. And to make matters even more challenging, the decision makers in almost all of these businesses were purchasing agents whose fathers were of the age that they had fought in World War II—against the Japanese. How would I get in the door? How could I possibly help them see a Japanese product in a different light? With the job at Vesco, rather than giving into skating by, I took on the difficulty of swaying reluctant buyers as a challenge. I distinctly remember when Bobby Byrd, another of the Vesco owners, held up one of my proposals in a sales meeting and told the assembled group, "This is what a world-class proposal looks like." I had fully thrown myself into the challenge and thought of every strategy I could for changing attitudes toward what I had come to know as a truly superior product.

What I saw as a challenge helped me begin to develop intrinsic motivation, though this was still true only within limits and without consistency. Even though I was successful at Vesco, I stayed for only a little over a year before I took another job selling material handling systems. I had quite a bit of success in this new role, but I still depended far too much on charisma and likability, and I was enamored with the accoutrements of success that were really quite shallow—a nice wardrobe, a new house, and a collection of clients who liked me. I fell into a pattern of doing enough to make the numbers, but I simply didn't perform to my potential, or my personal best, as John Wooden described it. Those habits didn't really change until I went to work for IBM. There I was able to observe the work habits of five key account representatives, the least senior of whom had been with the company for thirteen years. I respected them and didn't want to look amateurish in front of them. On my second day at work, the Greenville branch held a full-day meeting, during which I witnessed the award of a number of sales performance bonuses that were of a significant amount—more than any sales bonus I had ever received in my brief career. I decided right then and there that I didn't know how this worked but I was going to do whatever I had to do to get me some of that!

Shortly thereafter, I entered IBM's eighteen-month training program that included six three- or four-week classes, most of which were held in Las Colinas, Texas, but with one or two in New York at IBM headquarters. Throughout IBM training, each class elected officers (president, VP, secretary/treasurer), and everyone was ranked according to their performance in the class. Those rankings were reported back to your branch. My memory of those sales awards and my natural competitive spirit kicked in and motivated me for the first time in a professional setting to give my best and excel. The result was that I finished no worse than third in each of the three multiweek IBM training courses that I attended and completed. Of course, my performance was still somewhat extrinsically motivated—one sign of immaturity.

Slowly, I began to grow up. Those extrinsic motivators morphed, more and more, into a burgeoning desire to find satisfaction in *making* the sale rather than in worrying about the money I might make *from* the sale. I began to reflect on myself and my career and realized how much Dick Holdredge had taught me when he had challenged me for not fully learning the IBM product line or for anticipating what best served his company's needs. I learned to enjoy seeking out the opportunities that others avoided because they thought they would prove too hard. I began to anticipate changing markets rather than be surprised by them. I did more to apply my always present curiosity about an eclectic variety of topics to the work I was doing and the industry I had entered. Other habits changed too. I became the guy who unlocked and relocked the office because I arrived promptly every day at 7:30 a.m. and departed at 6:15 p.m. My friend Carl Sobocinski, who is the owner of the Table 301 Restaurant Group and one of the most active philanthropists in my hometown of Greenville, South Carolina, captures the root of this philosophy best when he says, "Excellence is not an act; it's a habit."

The lessons didn't always stick. At one point, I had become seriously interested in computer-aided design technologies, which were just emerging, and I had been chasing what would have been a large sale. On the day I learned that I had lost that sale, I decided to console myself with a round of golf. The next morning, arriving dutifully at seven thirty, I was surprised to find the office door unlocked and the lights on. Surprise turned to shock when I turned the corner to my office to find my boss, Frank Bellavia, sitting at my desk. Frank worked in Greenville, and I worked in Asheville, sixty miles away. His first words were, "You lied to me; I ought to fire you." We had talked by phone the day before when I learned I had lost the sale. I had told him I was on the road meeting with some of my other customers. Somehow (to this day I don't know how) he found out that I was playing golf. He told me that despite the customer telling us they had rejected our proposal, he had learned that they hadn't yet issued a purchase order to their chosen vendor. Frank said, "Instead of me firing you, you're going to find a way to make this sale."

We put our heads together and began to strategize how we could earn their business. Frank knew that the customer's primary decision maker was a member of the Biltmore Country Club in Asheville, where our systems engineering manager was also a member. Frank and I initiated a conversation about how we might show them that we understood their needs over a round of golf. This was in March 1984, and as fate would have it, a cluster of twenty-four tornados, including seven deadly ones that reached level four on the Enhanced Fujita Scale, wreaked havoc all over the South on the day that we were to play. The worst of the storms were concentrated south and east of us, and I will never know why Biltmore Country Club let us play golf that day, but they did! Lightning struck three trees in the Biltmore area while we were on the course, and I don't think I've ever been as soaked. And I don't know if it was the tense storm-battered atmosphere or good competition or well-timed drinks after the round, but the client we were trying to woo listened to us that day, and the adventure together opened a door for more conversations. Ultimately, it took thirteen months before we finally got the deal done, but once we did, they signed a purchase order for $1.3 million. The lesson that was initiated by Frank, one that was solidified by being chilled to the bone from golfing in a cold, driving rain, is that real selling starts when the customer says no. It took Frank, an extrinsic, and important, motivational force in my life, to make me invest the time, energy, and intelligence required to resurrect the sales opportunity that I should have had the maturity to pursue and close on my own. I had given up at the word *no*, whereas Frank wanted to learn why the prospect had arrived at this position and what could be done to change his mind. This one event in my life forever impressed upon me the understanding that real freedom isn't being able to do anything you *want* to do; freedom is having the power to do what you know you *ought* to do.

I absolutely value the lessons that people like Frank Bellavia and Dick Holdredge taught me, but I realized that I needed to depend upon myself to generate the intrinsic motivation required to make positive change a repetitive occurrence in my life. To do so inherently meant that I needed to push myself harder. I could not simply walk away at no. I learned the hard way that many times the things we want to do the least are the things we ought to do the most.

As I advanced to broader business and community leadership roles, my growing awareness and adoption of proven leadership principles was strongly reinforced when I read *Fail-Safe Leadership* by Linda L. Martin and David G. Mutchler, which argues that what long existed as the quintessential example of leadership, the charismatic leader, is bankrupt. Many times, charismatic leaders are great performers. It's costume leadership—theatrical drama—the sort that today seems to be regularly delivered by some of our politicians. In his book *Good to Great*, Jim Collins promoted the idea that charisma is more of a liability than an asset when it comes to leadership. I dub it the curse of charisma. If you don't achieve the desired end result, you can look the part, but you are not a real leader. Real leaders achieve the desired result the right way. They complete the mission. *Fail-Safe Leadership* promotes the premise that the only difference between a great performer and a great leader is *two words*. Great *performers* set goals and achieve results. Great *leaders* set goals and achieve results *through others.*

That last point found in *Fail-Safe Leadership*, that goals are realized via results through *others*, is a key point about maturity in a leader. David Wilkins, former US Ambassador to Canada and the former chair of Clemson University's Board of Trustees,

Real leaders achieve the desired result the right way.

captured this idea best when he modified John Maxwell's oft-quoted line by saying, "If you think you're leading and nobody's following, you're just taking a walk." Authentic leaders are teachers and coaches. When thinking about their impact in the organization and in the personal and professional lives of those in their orbit, authentic leaders ask, "Did I tell you something, show you something, give you something, or teach you something that you could easily put into practice and that, when you did, made your life better?" When leaders understand that the measure of their influence as a leader is not gauged by their success but by the successes of those around them, they realize why Jackie Robinson's epitaph reads "A life is not important except in the impact it has on others' lives." Jim Collins spoke to this principle by discussing how leaders multiply themselves through others. That mission is not accomplished by making people into carbon copies of yourself but by passing on principles, practices, and approaches that improve others' lives. They wear the mantle of leadership lightly and allow their subjects the freedom they need to make their own decisions, within limits. The best leaders also allow their subordinates to fail in a supportive environment so that they can learn from their experiences, but they also encourage their team to take risks that can lead to results.

All meaningful and lasting change starts first on the inside and works its way out. I don't know who said this, but I certainly ascribe to this philosophy. Once you begin to believe in yourself, you become intrinsically motivated. You don't need someone to push you; you propel yourself forward by second nature, realizing that the world is filled with opportunities, fascinating ideas, and interesting experiences. When you are unafraid of failure, within limits, you have a passion for taking on challenges that you would have previously sidestepped, many of which offer a path to measurable professional and personal success. Authentic leaders understand that leadership is about making your corner of the world better. Being committed to the cause of extending the gold standard by materially improving the current reality—through others—requires leaders to be unselfish and humble, which is another sign of leadership maturity and a key leadership trait we will explore in the next chapter.

MANTRAS FOR EXCELLENCE:

O Being right is overrated.

O Being together is more important than being right.

O Good leaders only have to be right 51 percent of the time. It just has to be the right 51 percent!

O "Let's do it your way."

O It doesn't matter if you're right or if I'm right. Let's just get it right.

O We are all doing so much these days that it feels like we're trying to cram ten pounds of potatoes into a five-pound sack.

O You can do the "right" thing in the wrong way or at the wrong time, and it can be worse than doing nothing at all.

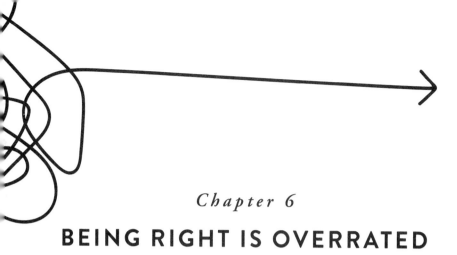

Chapter 6

BEING RIGHT IS OVERRATED

Everybody wants their star to shine the brightest. Everybody wants to have the right answer, every time. That's human nature. Sometimes leadership is about swimming against the tide. Mature leaders understand that being right is overrated. In fact, when you are a leader, if you are always "right," you may end up hurting those around you and cause harm to your organization. If you are the one who is always "right," over time you demoralize and demotivate those around you. Those whose ideas are never seriously considered or whose proposals don't regularly see the light of day feel invisible or believe they are pawns forced to pander to the ego of the person in charge, a person who may be the designated leader but who does not fully grasp the seriousness or significance of their actions upon the lives of those under their direction. People have a tendency to believe in the reality in which they find themselves. Historically, we promoted commercial cultures in which the boss was always right. In those legacy environments, subordinates looked to them as the primary or sole generator of ideas, and typically, under their breath they were saying, "What a

THE WINDING ROAD TO EXCELLENCE

chump. My ideas are so much better." When that's the case, even when you do have the best idea, it's never going to get implemented in an optimum fashion if those who must put it into action aren't inspired, even when the idea is the best approach. Someone once said, "Inspiration precedes perspiration," and I have learned that if you want to secure everyone's best effort, engage them at the ideation stage rather than at the implementation stage. Me being right constrains collaboration, dismisses others' ideas, limits creativity, breeds arrogance, puts others off, and makes me seem unapproachable. It creates a culture where my idea is best and yours is second best. Or worse, it makes your idea wrong. The smart leader realizes that there are times when being together is more important than being right.

Maybe you really do have the best idea most of the time. The following mantra originated with my late father-in-law, Don Ebert, who aptly summed up the reality of being the leader: Good leaders only have to be right 51 percent of the time. It just has to be the *right* 51 percent! Let's look at that in its full perspective. It may well be that the smoothest and fastest road to results is to implement your idea. But wise leaders know when to go all in and use the capital their position has provided them and when to sit out a hand and defer to others. In those instances when someone else has voiced an idea that will also achieve the desired results, the sense of pride and contribution they may feel is more than worth it, even if their idea adds two steps, takes two more days, or costs two more dollars. One of the most important five-word phrases that every leader must learn is this: "Let's do it your way."

Remember when I told you about the technology tours I ran in Europe when I was with Right Source? Well, success bred success, and six city tours became twelve city tours, and each one took us farther and farther afield. I had brought only a few Americans with me to

Europe, and we quickly needed to hire more help in the form of native language speakers and tour managers to plan and organize each roadshow that spanned multiple countries and venues. Early in our tenure in the Netherlands, we recruited a young Hollander, Cyriel Blezer, to serve in the role of show producer. But as our business expanded, we needed another tour manager, and Cyriel was the most experienced person at hand. I can't remember which tour it was, but I told Cyriel that he was going to be the tour manager and that he needed to come back to

> Wise leaders know when to go all in and use the capital their position has provided them and when to sit out a hand and defer to others.

me with a plan as to how he would staff and organize the tour. A couple of days later, Cyriel presented a fairly detailed plan for the tour. I reviewed the plan and found it very different from the way that we had organized tours in the US, especially from a travel and logistics perspective. The crisscrossing of countries on a regular basis looked very inefficient to me. I told Cyriel, "I am not sure this is going to work. The plan you have concocted is completely different from the way in which we ran these tours in the US. I just don't see how this approach is practical. I can think of two or three better ways that I would organize this project."

Cyriel replied, "Toby, no disrespect, but you're not from Europe. This isn't like the United States. Europe is not fifty states with the same language, same culture, same customs, and same transportation systems. The presentations, venue, and catering will need to align with the culture, customs, and tastes of each location. And we need to sequence events according to the language that will be used in the presentation, not by the proximity of the venues to each other.

The people I've put on my team understand the fact that Europe is a collection of very diverse countries and environments, and they will make this work."

I asked Cyriel to let me sleep on his proposal. The next morning, I told him, "I still don't know if you're right or not, but one thing I do know is that you seem absolutely convinced your plan will work. I've decided to let you run this tour your way, but you dadgum better be right." The end result was that the tour that Cyriel organized was one of the most profitable we ever ran. My experience with Cyriel and that tour taught me a lesson—a mantra—that I have never forgotten: It doesn't matter if you're right or if I'm right. Let's just get it right.

The areas in life and in business in which we can truly be an expert get *narrower* every day. There's so much science, so much technology, so much math, so much design, and so much intelligence in every discipline that we can only be truly expert in a few things. Couple that reality with the fact that we are all trying to do so much these days that it feels like we're trying to cram ten pounds of potatoes into a five-pound sack. So we have to rely on subject matter experts to distill information for us and guide us toward educated decisions because we can't know it all, and even those who are the very best at what they do can't do it all.

It doesn't matter if you're right or if I'm right. Let's just get it right.

BMW Manufacturing operates a vehicle assembly plant halfway between Greenville and Spartanburg, South Carolina. Every X Series Sports Activity Vehicle (SAV) that BMW produces for worldwide consumption is *assembled* in that facility. Notice that I said assembled, even though the owner and operator of the plant is BMW Manufacturing. The reality is that BMW doesn't fully manufacture the ultimate driving machine—they *assemble* it. BMW manufactures some of the best auto bodies and engines in the world, but that is the extent of the primary components that BMW actually manufactures for its line of X Series vehicles. From there they turn to the expertise of others, like ZF for transmissions, Draexlmaier for interior systems, Bilstein for shock absorbers, Michelin for tires, and Harman Kardon for sound systems. Seen this way, BMW is actually a design, systems integration, testing, assembly, marketing, sales, distribution, and service organization, not just a vehicle manufacturing company. Like or unlike BMW, you may or may not outsource entire components of your business the way a modern automobile manufacturer does, but you had better learn when to secure and incorporate the knowledge and expertise of others if you want to produce consistently stellar results.

When you draw upon the experience and expertise of a diverse, capable, dedicated group around you, the more you and all of your team feel valued and motivated. When team members' ideas are heard and implemented, they take pride in their work. They see the enterprise as an extension of themselves. To excel, an organization needs leaders who inspire others to extraordinary performance. If we inspire others only to match the level of performance that is widely accepted as the gold standard in our market space, we will never extend the current standard of excellence. We do not want to simply compete in the markets that we serve; we want to "sur-pete," to quote Dr. Edward de Bono, the author of *Sur-Petition*. In other words, we must *surpass* the performance of our peers, becoming not only thought leaders but also executional and operational leaders. Only then can we optimize our performance.

> To excel, an organization needs leaders who inspire others to extraordinary performance.

Once we set our standards to the highest levels achievable, we begin to recognize subtler realities, such as you can do the "right" thing in the wrong way or at the wrong time, and it can be worse than doing nothing at all. Objectives shift. Priorities change. Unexpected challenges arise. Ultimately, what is "right" is the thing that produces tangible results…in the right way. Wrong means do not justify the right result.

Accepting the premise that being right is overrated requires humility. Next, we'll explore why being humble is essential for anyone focused on getting results and drawing the best performance out of those around them.

MANTRAS FOR EXCELLENCE:

○ Humility is more important than visibility.

○ Concentrate on paying attention rather than on drawing attention.

○ There's plenty of sunshine to go around; make sure others get to stand in the brightest spot sometimes.

○ "Good leadership is the ideal blend of extreme personal humility and intense professional will." —Jim Collins

○ "It's my fault. Blame me."

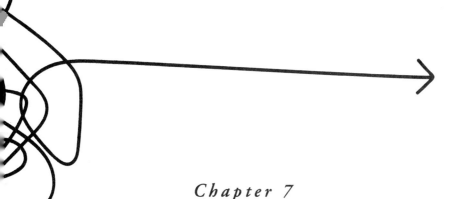

Chapter 7

HUMILITY IS MORE IMPORTANT THAN VISIBILITY

When I was president of OOBE, for no particular reason except that I happened to be thinking about some of my conversations with employees that day, I grabbed a marker and wrote the following phrase on one of the flip charts in our conference room: Criticism provides an opportunity for improvement. I came back into that same room the next day and found that someone had added the word *constructive* before *criticism*. This alteration didn't hit me exactly right. It took me a while to decipher why, but I came to the conclusion that the recipients of criticism are often more concerned with the source, motive, or tone of the criticism than with the content. It dawned on me that we may unconsciously filter or dismiss what we hear based not upon the legitimacy and value of the information but upon the source, motivation, and tone of the delivery. It would seem that our attitude in these instances may actually retard our pace of learning, as it roadblocks any knowledge that might be delivered in a manner that doesn't emotionally suit us. I don't know a lot, but I do know that in competitive business environments with individuals at all levels vying for significance, value, position, and money, not all criticism is offered with the purest of motives or the sweetest of tones. Some misguided criticism stems from jealousy, some from competitiveness, some from insecurity, and some from just plain old meanness. And yes, some criticism does originate from individuals who truly are trying to help us achieve our full potential as employees and as human beings. But the ratio of the Pareto principle (80 percent of outcomes stem from 20 percent of causes) probably applies to this phenomenon as it does in many other situations. I have no data to justify this position, but I wouldn't be surprised if 80 percent of all criticism is delivered with a less than ideal approach and with an intent to hurt more than help.

I would submit that someone who maintains an attitude of receptivity when receiving criticism from another individual, regardless of how it is delivered, will learn and grow faster than one who goes deaf when the approach used by the messenger is impolite, rude, vindictive, or inappropriate. Many years ago, I learned to turn off all filters when criticism comes my way. I try to take it all in and to offer no reaction to the messenger except to thank them for sharing what they observed, what they think, and how they feel. Then, when I am alone, I review all the points made and try to objectively evaluate the validity of what was shared. If I am fortunate, I find truth in the message that helps me recognize shortcomings of which I may have been unaware or simply didn't want to admit. Those discoveries provide an immediate opportunity to learn and grow. They also provide a chance to circle back to the person who delivered the criticism and to thank them for helping me see where I could improve. It really doesn't matter if 80 percent of what they told me was rubbish and completely untrue; I try to concentrate on the 20 percent that can be leveraged to increase my knowledge, productivity, and impact. Experience has taught me that there is nearly always something instructive and prescriptive in well-intentioned criticism—in, dare I say it, constructive criticism. That reminder of my reaction to my altered flip chart suggests something more revealing: how often I have managed to remain blind to valid criticism, ignored it, or actively avoided it. While it's true that we can all be our own harshest critics, it's simultaneously true that we all have blind spots, those underdeveloped parts of our personalities we don't care to reveal or that we are reluctant to change. To accept that we always have more to learn, including learning more about *ourselves*, requires humility. In order to benefit from others' criticism, well intentioned or otherwise, you have to learn to concentrate on paying attention rather than on drawing attention.

I've spoken before about the myopic nature of traditional leadership models where the leader is placed (or places themselves) on a pedestal and declares that their ideas alone form the manifesto we must all follow. The supposedly infallible leader who bases their leadership on power and charisma never offers much actual value, as common sense will tell us. Even if a leader is experienced and highly intelligent, what are the odds that they consistently have the one right answer? How often is there only one answer? When the *Apollo 13* mission to the moon suffered an explosion that threatened its crew's ability to return home to Earth, do you think it was only Jim Lovell, the mission commander, and mission control's flight director, Gene Kranz, who proposed every idea, every improvised solution, every bit of math and technology and gadget wizardry necessary to get the crew home safely? Those two may have managed

> To accept that we always have more to learn, including learning more about *ourselves*, requires humility.

the crisis masterfully, but it took the whole of NASA working together to find all the factored solutions. Kranz understood that his team as a whole was greater than the sum of its individual parts and instructed them to take ownership of their specialist areas, to collaborate and to be creative and innovative in their approach to problem-solving. When we pay attention rather than draw attention, we move our enterprises toward opportunities and through the problem-solving process to arrive at substantive conclusions.

The importance of paying attention extends beyond looking outward toward others rather than only inward to the self; it becomes a mantra for all of living—seeing what is going on around us by being truly awake. This means truly listening to people, hearing their words but also understanding their context, whether that is an outreach from a friend who may be going through a difficult period or an employee who is handed conventional approaches and established processes that are unwieldy or ineffective. In our professional lives, it means paying attention to what's going on around us in the market, within our company, and with our competition. Talk to people, do some research, listen to the people in your organization who are comfortable telling you the things you don't want to hear, make it easy for your customers to tell you about the likes and dislikes they found in the experience of doing business with your company. Seek out reliable information and open your eyes to the implications it holds for the needs of your business.

The combination of staying focused enough to pay attention and humble enough not to draw attention is at the heart of a let's-do-it-your-way mentality. There's plenty of sunshine to go around; make sure others get to stand in the brightest spot sometimes. As Jim Collins taught us, good leadership is the ideal blend of extreme personal humility and intense professional will. The trick is translating those characteristics into actionable, prescriptive instructions that can be executed by every individual in your company in a manner that makes a measurable difference in the top and bottom lines on the income statement. Translation starts by taking the spotlight off yourself and putting it on those doing the actual work, particularly those who have the most direct contact with your customers and those at the heart of your processes. The consistent message that has to be promoted in word and played out in deed is this: "It's not about me; it's about you."

When you see genuine humility in a leader firsthand, it can be life changing. That is not an exaggeration, and I can share an experience that illustrates that reality in spades. I have been fortunate to meet and get to know many humble leaders, but one person epitomizes this quality: Randy Dobbs. Randy entered my life as a total stranger. When I was the president of OOBE, we not only produced OOBE branded apparel, but we also designed and produced apparel for the Wolverine brand. One of our cofounder's best friends was the tournament director for the BMW Charity Pro-Am golf tournament, which at the time was played on three courses spread across Upstate South Carolina and western North Carolina. We reached an agreement for OOBE to serve as the official apparel provider for the tournament, outfitting all the volunteers, stewards, officials, and others. As part of our sponsorship agreement, OOBE was able to have two foursomes play in the tournament, so we invited a couple of Wolverine executives and two OOBE executives to partner with the two pros who played in each foursome. Because most people see me when I'm giving an economic development presentation, teaching a course, or running a meeting, and because I have had the privilege of working closely with a number of Greenville's civic leaders, most people assume I'm a fairly outgoing extrovert. In truth, I'm introspective by nature and I like my alone time, especially on the weekends. One unseasonably chilly early Saturday morning in May during the tournament, I found some alone time while supporting the two OOBE/Wolverine teams by following our two foursomes who happened to be playing at Bright's Creek, the North Carolina course. I'd positioned myself between the two foursomes and was standing alone just off the green of the third hole waiting for the second foursome to play through. The tournament didn't attract a lot of spectators early in the morning on such a cool day, so the crowd was sparse, and I was enjoying some thinking time. After our first foursome completed the hole, three women and a tall lanky guy came walking up the third fairway toward the green where I was standing. I assumed they were related to the pros in the foursome. However, the lanky guy sidled up to me and initiated a conversation. He was extremely nice, friendly, and low key, but I had been enjoying the quiet and kind of wished he would continue on with the women and leave me to my thoughts. He asked who I was with among the golfers, and I told him about OOBE's affiliation to the tournament. As the golfers moved on to the next hole, he politely asked if he might tag along.

Chatting as we walked, we started with the usual questions you ask as you get to know someone. He told me he was from Arkansas and that he grew up in Alabama. He had a southern accent nearly as strong as my own. I asked him what he did for a living, and he just said, "Oh, I've done a lot of different things, you know. Some private equity work in New York. I've done some work in the medical field." He never got specific. He told me about his two kids in Atlanta. He was easy to talk with and pleasant. When we got to the ninth hole, he asked, "You hungry? I'm a member here, and they're doing a nice brunch today at the clubhouse. You want to join me?" Genuinely enjoying his company despite my initial reluctance, I readily agreed.

We talked through lunch. We talked through the next nine holes while walking the course. We talked as we sat in the spectator stands on the eighteenth hole. I've never become such instant friends with someone in my life. I felt like I had known Randy forever. When I got home, I looked him up and was shocked to find that he had been the CEO of three different companies that operated on a global basis. Randy had led GE Capital, IT Systems, Phillips Medical Systems, and United States Investigative Services. He is the author of *Transformational Leadership: A Blueprint for Real Organizational Change,* which details proven strategic business tools and transformational leadership. I was floored. Here was this humble, approachable, ordinary guy who had accomplished so much. Randy has been among my closest friends ever since that golf tournament. We've spent time together in each other's homes, call one another with regularity, and have shared some of the most important elements of our lives through stories about our families and about the beliefs that drive us.

Randy fulfills something that I have noticed about people across my lifetime. Some you meet and you're instantly blown away by their energy and intelligence and passion, and more often than not, over time you realize that all you saw during that first meeting is most of what's there; those people ultimately tend to disappoint you. On the other hand, often it is those people who you see as interesting and earnest but who don't make a grand first impression that, as you come to know them better and better, continue to grow in stature and reveal more layers about themselves and tremendous depth in their knowledge and interests. They don't make a big deal about themselves because they truly are humble at the core of their being. They don't see themselves as big deals. The people in this latter group tend to fulfill what Jim Collins called level five leadership, that paradoxical combination of extreme personal humility and intense professional will. People like Randy and like all of the most important people in my life are never trying to draw attention. They are paying attention. They live by the meaning of Philippians 2:3, which says, "Let nothing be done through selfish ambition or conceit, but in lowliness of mind, let each esteem others better than himself."

Randy is the epitome of a humble leader. One natural part of being humble is the ability to admit when you have made mistakes. My wife's refusal to let me use the word *mistake* closely parallels Dad's guidance from an earlier era in my life. When I was a teenager, he used to tell me, "Toby, you are competitive and assertive by nature, which means you're gonna do some dumb things you wish you hadn't done. You're gonna screw up. All I ask is that you own it when you do." I've already shared with you one of the most important five-word sentences you will ever learn: "Let's do it your way"; it's corresponding partner five-word sentence is "It's my fault. Blame me." This is an essential trait in leaders. If people don't know that you are fallible, then you will never be approachable. An unapproachable leader is one who is cut off from their organization. And such a leader will never be able to create a culture where others will take responsibility for their own actions. An ability to admit when I am wrong helps me value others and their perspectives and makes me listen better. Just as we need to be able to admit our bad choices, we have to acknowledge when our tactics are ineffective and we lose out on a contract or fail to land or keep a customer. If we're not willing to simply say, "I got beat," we're not willing to get better. By the way, it's probably worth mentioning that the second piece of my dad's advice was this: "Make sure you don't make the same mistake [or bad choice, as Susan calls it] twice," which is pretty sage advice.

Being humble is made easier if leaders realize their most important job is to generate new leaders. The leader should not seek attention or award for their own efforts or achievements, for ultimately the only measurement of a leader's success that matters resides in our ability to help others achieve theirs. It is a leader's job to help every employee succeed. *My signature question is this: "What can I do to help you?"* That question is at the heart of humility, but it has to be genuine. It's a loaded question because you might not be prepared for how someone is going to answer it, yet you have to be prepared to do what they ask. Anything short of that and you have simply created the specter of leadership through

> **Being humble is made easier if leaders realize their most important job is to generate new leaders.**

your words, but you have omitted the essential execution component. The leadership model you have created is in reality a facade, and if there is anything employees can see in their leaders, it's when they are faking it.

Humility isn't so difficult if you genuinely care about others. What can be hard, however, is to develop the humility to look at yourself with total honesty—warts and all—hear the accurate criticisms of others—those honest constructive attempts to cut through any facade that does exist—and act on your failures and foibles. Only then are you capable of honestly evaluating your own weaknesses—something that is essential for any leader—and this includes what may be your greatest weakness, which is where we go next.

MANTRAS FOR EXCELLENCE:

o Your greatest weakness is many times an unprotected or misguided strength.

o The world today rewards mental and physical agility as much as it rewards experience.

o Extraordinary performance stems from regular, incremental improvement.

o Wise people learn from experience. Wiser people learn from the experiences of others.

o If it's broken, then fix it...or kill it.

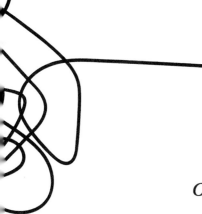

Chapter 8

YOUR GREATEST
WEAKNESS MAY BE AN
UNPROTECTED STRENGTH

Being able to admit your weaknesses is one aspect of humility. Humility is largely about self-honesty. Don't look in the mirror to admire yourself but to truly see yourself. There are some parts of ourselves our egos risk having us never see. Real introspection means that we can learn to separate ego (our sense of self-esteem or self-importance) from our ego strength (the part that allows us to say, "I can do this no matter how hard it is or how foreign it seems"); then we become capable of cutting through all the armor we tend to wear and see our weaknesses. Here's the reality: your greatest weakness is many times an unprotected or misguided strength.

I introduced this mantra at the outset of the book because it is so important. It's worth repeating one more time: Your greatest weakness is many times an unprotected or misguided strength. What are you *not* seeing when you look in the mirror? What skill, knowledge, or talent do you possess and promote that was once the sharpest tool in the toolbox but is now rusting away in the corner? What are those things for which you are known as having a great perspective or the ideal solution and about which your reputation is that you've got it all figured out? Maybe you had the perfect solution once, at that particular moment or across a limited time span. Just because you had it figured out once, that doesn't mean much in the world in which we live now. In a dynamic world that changes as quickly as it does today, that effectiveness of the perfect solution begins eroding the day that we first discovered it. That erosion can quickly transform a strength into a weakness. It may not be the wrong solution today, but it's misguided to blindly believe that what worked in the past will work as well today or in the future. We have to stay current to remain relevant. And staying current takes curiosity and effort.

If you spoke with most CEOs in late 2019, my bet is that they would have expressed confidence in the reliability and quality of their suppliers and supply network. Most would have said, "We've got our supply chain all figured out." It wouldn't matter what industry they were in. They would proudly point to deals they had made for critical supplies at low costs, how they had wisely invested in sophisticated software that monitored and dynamically managed lead times for tight turnarounds. Accurate demand, lead time, and logistics data enabled many organizations to maintain raw materials, component, subassembly, and finished goods inventories at increasingly lean levels and maximize inventory turns,

> **We have to stay current to remain relevant.**

which then freed up cash for other initiatives and investments. Then bam! Enter 2020. If you talked to the same CEOs in the fall of 2020, the majority would have readily acknowledged that the belief that they had mastered their supply chains was a quite serious case of putting stock in an unprotected strength. They had been severely duped because they thought they had it all figured out, but they had failed to ask the necessary what-if questions that would force them to build contingency plans for the truly unexpected. I would go a step further and propose that while COVID-19 did in fact *create* monumental supply chain challenges, it also *revealed* a host of issues that were already lurking just below the surface in a globally intertwined system of supply. The problems we are dealing with today were decades in the making. The old adage of if it ain't broke, don't fix it doesn't apply anymore. We must be intrinsically motivated and self-managed to hypothesize, develop, deploy, and operate better processes, introduce better solutions, and build a more reliable and redundant supply network *before* our customers or the competition or another virus force us to do so. If we did it yesterday and we need to do it today, then it's important to find a better way, today and every day.

You put new tires on your vehicle when the tread starts to wear down because you recognize that you need great traction in all weather conditions, but you don't change out the driveshaft just because you can, and you don't stop driving because you fear the wear and tear that comes with every commute. If somebody offers you an amazing opportunity but you're not sure you can do it, say yes, then learn how to do it as you go. You have to keep developing as a person and you have to keep developing as a company. We cannot become complacent. The world today rewards mental and physical agility as much as it rewards experience. If the old way really is working, then you're probably not even talking about it because success breeds complacency. Historically, the time to craft new solutions is when the old ones don't work anymore. In today's highly competitive, rapidly changing commercial landscape, you're too late if you follow that approach.

We have to learn how to turn loose of many ideas and approaches with which we are comfortable and to which we like to hold tight. Turn loose of our egos. Turn loose of our pride. Turn loose of our fear. We've got to turn loose of our belief that we've got all the right answers or that we've got it all figured out. Really, it is a matter of applying a simple principle to our own perceptions and actions, that extraordinary performance stems from regular, incremental improvement.

So how do we seize opportunity? How do we create changing solutions for changing times? That's where we apply the four As model. Similar to some of the acronyms I use, this approach is a *progression* of steps.

We start by being early adopters. That not only means a focus upon research and development, the output of which may be radically new approaches, products, or solutions, but also, and far more often, it means finding something that already exists elsewhere or is employed in a different application and adopting it. Then you adapt it to your needs. The vast majority of innovation isn't found in coming up with an entirely new idea; it's found in adapting ideas and solutions that are already in service somewhere in the world, sometimes in unrelated fields, to unique requirements that exist in your particular industry or company. In 1979, when Steve Jobs visited his neighbor Xerox PARC, he saw a number of innovations the Xerox engineers were working on with the Alto personal computer, but it was the graphical user interface that made him see what he believed would forever change all computing. He challenged his Apple engineers to adapt the principles of the graphical user interface and then vastly improved on it and made it more approachable and usable for consumers. He took something that existed and made it better. Adopting existing ideas and then adapting them to your specific situation and needs allows you to become effective faster. Because of the competitive nature of market participants within a single industry, this sort of adoption/adaptation is many times more prevalent interindustry than it is within an industry vertical.

Adoption and adaptation have become easier than ever. We have a world of potential solutions at our fingertips. We make it a standard practice to look externally for solutions when we understand that wise people learn from experience. Wiser people learn from the experiences of others.

Through adaptation, you speed up your ability to apply what you have adopted. You put it to work and see how it performs. Get your idea out into the field, then be intentional about assessing how it works. Make the necessary adjustments to optimize it to your needs. Make it work better. If a debrief after application reveals that it's broken, then fix it…or kill it.

Placing your enterprise in a position to apply the four As model starts with seeing and admitting that the changing climates in which we operate require us to acknowledge the need for the first *A*: adoption. We must adopt new ideas, strategies, and approaches or we risk becoming irrelevant, or worse, obsolete. Failure to do so is far more serious than hiding within our I've-got-it-figured-out armor. If we ignore this principle, we become guilty of outright arrogance.

The four As model is essential for an organization to attain and sustain excellence. Yet it is not enough. True excellence is achieved when you can begin to anticipate the needs of the future before they arrive. We have to learn to anticipate changing markets and shifting culture and act *before* they are broadly recognized and acknowledged by the rest of the

> True excellence is achieved when you can begin to anticipate the needs of the future before they arrive.

world. Even while we are in the final stages of making adjustments, wise leaders are always asking, "What's next?"

Will all of our predictions be right? Hardly. Will all of our adjustments work? Not likely. But we have to try. If we don't, we give in to our real weakness. And that weakness will not be found in failure, for it is in failure where we find our greatest lessons, as we will discuss in the next chapter.

MANTRAS OF EXCELLENCE:

O You very seldom learn something new when you experience repeated success. If you achieve success in an endeavor, you will generally execute the same process in the same way the next time you encounter a similar challenge. When you experience failure, you are forced to discover better ways to execute.

O "Doubt kills dreams more than failure ever will." —Suzy Kassem

O "Always make new mistakes." —Esther Dyson

O Failure is an early indicator of impending success.

O If you trust someone's motives, you're willing to forgive their mistakes.

O "Trials and tribulations don't build character; they reveal it." —Roger Neely

O Don't not try.

O "If what I did yesterday looks big to me, then I probably haven't done much today." —Lou Holtz

O "The worst kind of failure is to succeed at something that doesn't really matter." —Patrick Morley

Chapter 9

FAILURE IS AN EARLY INDICATOR OF IMPENDING SUCCESS

When we are genuinely humble and have learned to check our egos at the door, then we become keenly aware of and sensitive to the fact that new approaches and lessons are all around us if we will just keep our eyes and ears open and be receptive. The sad reality is that you very seldom learn something new when you experience repeated success. If you achieve success in an endeavor, you will generally execute the same process the same way the next time you encounter a similar challenge. When that happens, you've given into an unprotected or misguided strength. Guess what? That same "successful" process is unlikely to work as well, even if the next challenge is similar. By comparison to the minor lessons awaiting us in analyzing our successes, when you experience failure, you are forced to discover better ways to execute. When I have failed, and that has been often, my first reaction is almost always, "I'm not doing that again!" In 1921, Thomas Edison was interviewed by B. C. Forbes for *American Magazine*, in which he was quoted as saying,

> I never allow myself to become discouraged under any circumstances. I recall that after we had conducted thousands of experiments on a certain project without solving the problem, one of my associates, after we had conducted the crowning experiment and it had proved a failure, expressed discouragement and disgust over our having failed "to find out anything." I cheerily assured him that we had learned something. For we had learned for a certainty that the thing couldn't be done that way, and that we would have to try some other way. We sometimes learn a lot from our failures if we have put into the effort the best thought and work we are capable of.[1]

I don't think it is a stretch to say that NASA would not have experienced the success they did on *Apollo* missions 14, 15, 16, and 17 were it not for overcoming the nearly catastrophic failure of *Apollo 13*.

Of course, failing isn't easy, not on the psyche or on self-confidence. Yet if we are striving instead of settling, we will always encounter some degree of failure. I have tried to challenge every team I have ever led to identify their purpose and then become better than anyone else at accomplishing that purpose. We *cannot* allow the fear of failure to cause us to stop pushing. Doubt kills dreams more than failure ever will.[2]

I am sure my reputation in some quarters is that my philosophies and approaches might be considered somewhat unconventional. But

---

1   Interview between Thomas Edison and B. C. Forbes, *American Magazine*, January 1921.

2   Suzy Kassem, *Rise Up and Salute the Sun: The Writings of Suzy Kassem* (Awakened Press, 2011).

when it comes to failure, my perspectives are definitely unconventional, for beyond believing that we can learn from it, I think a failure to fail means we aren't attempting the things that are worth trying. It takes big dreams to accomplish big things, and it demands meaningful innovation, the sort we equate with reshaping and rethinking the very bedrock of convention. When Jeff Bezos first started Amazon, his business model was viewed as so unconventional that many found it crazy. And to focus on selling books was crazier still. Indeed, it took six years for Amazon to turn its first profit. Bezos saw something few others did, and he, like a number of other dot-com entrepreneurs, never interpreted the inability to turn a profit in the first few years of existence as a fatal blow to the future success of the organization. One of my favorite quotes is from Esther Dyson, the investor, journalist, author, and philanthropist: "Always make new mistakes." It is only when we are testing the edge and thinking in new patterns that we experience the breakthroughs that become transformative. You can't make new mistakes if you are not trying new things. In fact, I like to turn convention about failure on its head and frequently say that failure is an early indicator of impending success.

> A failure to fail means we aren't attempting the things that are worth trying.

So long as the risks you take in pursuit of excellence don't violate the six Cs—catastrophically harming the company, our culture, an important customer, a significant contract, your character, or your confidence—and you have kept the company's core ideology at the center of your thinking and behavior, you're unlikely to experience the kind of failure from which you can't recover or one that won't produce far greater rewards in the lessons it teaches or in the realities that it reveals.

If you trust someone's motives, you're willing to forgive their mistakes. Some mistakes carry bigger consequences than others and will result in trials you will have to endure, but you will come out the other side stronger, and you will learn more about your company culture and your team's ability to pull together. As Roger Neely, our business applications manager when I was at OOBE and still a good friend of mine to this day, once astutely said, "Trials and temptations don't build character; they reveal it." If we are to grow into authentic leaders, we will need the type of character that will drive us to dissect our failures and extract valuable lessons that will positively impact our future. Put in the simplest language, I fully subscribe to this piece of advice that I first encountered through the American Hydrocephalus Association: don't not try.

> If we are to grow into authentic leaders, we will need the type of character that will drive us to dissect our failures and extract valuable lessons that will positively impact our future.

When we pursue excellence, we push up against limits that have previously not been penetrated. We venture into new terrain. We set our sights beyond what appears on the horizon. To pursue excellence, we are committed to surpassing what has been achieved before. As legendary football coach Lou Holtz said, "If what I did yesterday looks big to me, then I probably haven't done much today." I simply don't think we can ever achieve excellence if we don't *project*—i.e., look ahead—and extend our reach. When you place tall hurdles in front of yourself, you're going to trip once in a while. Get up. Dust yourself off. Assess what went wrong. Then have another go at it. What I won't do is invest all my effort into something that holds no real importance. I'm in full agreement with Patrick Morley, the founder of Man in the Mirror, when he said, "The worst kind of failure is to succeed at something that doesn't really matter."[3]

Everything I have discussed in this chapter has focused on fixable failures. Most of the fixes I have addressed have been about fixing our own character and shifting our perspective. In the next chapter, I will discuss building on strength of character, pursuing moral imperatives, and applying the kinds of lessons we learn when things don't go quite according to plan.

---

3   Patrick Morley, "Nine Things You Need to Know to "Pastor" Men Effectively," Man in the Mirror, December 10, 2008. .

MANTRAS FOR EXCELLENCE:

O   Most of us make decisions emotionally and then build a case to support them rationally.

O   You can teach an animal right from wrong, but you can only teach a human wise from unwise.

O   Go to the source. Secondhand information is rarely as accurate as that which you can obtain from the author or perpetrator.

O   Delay is the deadliest five-letter word in the English language.

Chapter 10

RESPONSIBLE DECISION-MAKING

The past several chapters have all, in one fashion or another, focused on essential aspects of character. While qualities like intrinsic motivation, lifelong learning, humility, and confidence without egotism are vital to leaders, I think they are important to everyone, and they apply equally in our professions and in our private lives. All these qualities must be brought to bear when we are faced with tough decisions.

Most of us reading this book have convinced ourselves that we are intelligent and informed individuals who make logical, well-intentioned decisions based upon data and experience. Au contraire, my friend. My observation is that most of us make decisions emotionally and then build a case to support them rationally. We construct rational justifications for what we *want* to do and make excuses for what we shouldn't have done. We need to instill a business culture that facilitates the opposite, where we intellectualize our decision-making and do so based upon reliable data. However, we should not become robotic in our decisions, nor do I want to play it safe by taking the easy way out when there is ground to be gained by taking a calculated risk. I rely on a decision-making approach that leverages experience, historical data, and reliable and logical predictive data that help us identify and quantify formidable challenges as well as highly lucrative opportunities. I heard this approach called data-informed intuition, and I think that is an accurate moniker. I want to carefully capture, organize, assess, and leverage all the relevant data, but I don't want to discard my past experiences and my gut feeling when making decisions. At Cargo, our decision-making equation is this: Evidence-based intelligence (data) + Experience-based insights (lessons learned) = Prescriptive guidance.

Beyond this approach, we also can be more confident in our decisions when they are grounded in our core values of right and wrong, doing good for others, being truthful, offering clarity, and delivering impeccable quality that *exceeds* the customers' expectations. When our decisions are congruent with our personal values, we begin to develop and exhibit mature judgment and wisdom beyond right and wrong that enables us to effectively navigate truly complex decisions with a level of acumen and foresight that is truly rare these days.

You can teach an animal right from wrong, but you can only teach a human wise from unwise. There are plenty of things that are not necessarily wrong, but they're not wise. Determining the difference requires an elevated level of discernment and is a trait that is exhibited by the best leaders. The best leaders make the best decisions. It's that simple. Wisdom is in short supply and is a rare quality these days, but it is essential to maximizing your ability to influence and impact other people. Sadly, I have found that teaching our dog not to go to the bathroom in the house is a whole lot easier than getting people to recognize the difference between rightness and wisdom. The problem with making purely data-driven decisions is that there is simply too much information and too much to know. In fact, there is so much information available in the world today about every subject and discipline that the areas of life or business in which we can truly claim to be an expert get *narrower* every day. While C-level leaders need to be generalists by nature and must possess an awareness and understanding of a broad range of subjects that enable them to integrate disparate ideas, processes, and technologies,

The best leaders make the best decisions. It's that simple.

they also must rely on an internal and external community of subject matter experts who possess an elevated level of knowledge and expertise in a number of niche disciplines. Leaders must be prepared to ask such experts probing questions, listen to their answers and their informed opinions, and then make decisions that integrate those specialized expert perspectives into solutions that synthesize with dozens, if not hundreds, of other moving parts.

We all encounter situations in which it is challenging to determine what really happened. As my dad told me one time, "The truth just isn't that easy to figure out, so let's stick to the facts." When you find yourself in the middle of such an occurrence, information generally floods in from all directions, and it becomes challenging to discern the sequence of events and who said what to whom. Because the truth is not that easy to extract or discern, remember this: Go to the source. Secondhand information is rarely as accurate as that which you can obtain from the author or perpetrator. We are all too familiar with how rumors move through an organization, no matter its size. Too often people begin to act on such misinformation. When in doubt, find the origin or turn to the expert and have a direct conversation. Don't make assumptions or take action based upon innuendos or unsubstantiated facts.

You can delegate authority, but you can never delegate responsibility. You must own your decisions. Decisions are informed by the expertise of others, but your decisions are not made by others. So what do you do when those confidants are not available, or you have no one with whom you can collaborate as you face a decision? That is why I opened the chapter as I did: You must be comfortable and confident in your own judgment. Trust your values and trust your instincts, don't react with emotion, keep the six Cs firmly in mind, and make the decision. Don't delay. *Delay* is the deadliest five-letter word in the English language. If you have a bad disease and you delay seeing a doctor, your condition will deteriorate because of your indecision. Your condition certainly won't improve, and if you delay too long, the consequences could be disastrous. Make a decision and take action. Paraphrased, the German field marshal known as Moltke the Elder said, "No battle plan survives first contact with the enemy." Mike Tyson, former heavyweight champion boxer said, "Everyone has a plan until they get punched in the mouth." Everything doesn't turn out like we want. Plan accordingly. If it doesn't work out like you thought it would, deal with it; don't defend it.

Don't make assumptions or take action based upon innuendos or unsubstantiated facts.

When you are *not* in a situation in which you have to face a difficult decision alone—and in a well-staffed organization, you should have at your disposal colleagues who can offer accurate, reliable, collaborative input—then you need to learn how to solicit and manage in an expedient fashion the breadth of expertise and experience that is available from others. That's why you must master some other Cs, four of them to be exact, as I will discuss next.

MANTRAS FOR EXCELLENCE:

O   We need to know how to step on people's toes without taking the shine off their shoes.

O   "Get better, not bitter." —Roger Neely

O   It's one thing to be a great leader; it's another thing to be a great leader on a great team.

Chapter 11

THE FOUR Cs OF TEAMWORK

I returned to Greenville, South Carolina, in 2004 and became president of OOBE in 2006. I soon thereafter became involved in the Greenville Chamber of Commerce and a number of other education, healthcare, and economic development groups and projects, including my first opportunity working with the wonderful entrepreneurs who matriculated through the Greenville Chamber's Minority Business Accelerator. I love the city of Greenville and value living in a thriving, forward-thinking community. For many years, the Greenville Chamber of Commerce, in collaboration with Clemson University, assimilated an economic scorecard that measured the city's economic status in a comparative analysis with other southern peer cities like Durham, North Carolina; Jacksonville, Florida; and Birmingham, Alabama. In 2009, the results of that comparison showed that while per capita personal income in Greenville was growing, our growth trajectory paled in comparison to our sister cities and had done so for a number of years. The chamber took it upon itself to survey a group of fifty or so CEOs and presidents of companies that were located within the greater Greenville area to discuss potential initiatives that could stimulate job and income growth and attract new commercial and industrial ventures. When the chamber leaders asked for my suggestions for improving the status quo, I said, "I'd get more companies like BMW to locate here." While employing more polite terms, many of my fellow leaders and chamber colleagues inferred that was the dumbest thing they had ever heard. BMW had built the first plant outside of Germany in Upstate South Carolina in 1995, and while it had been a tremendous success and had seen incredible growth, my associates rightly saw that the possibility of landing another automobile assembly plant in the upstate area of South Carolina was virtually nonexistent. "You've got the wrong idea," I said. "Let me explain. If we can get other companies—the industry doesn't matter—to come here that operate a just-in-time manufacturing model like a car manufacturer does, not only will they locate their company here but also they will drag their supply base with them. We want to attract industries that need their suppliers and distribution network in close proximity to the mother ship. That will create a multiplication effect that spawns job creation and economic impact on a broad scale." They saw the wisdom of what I was describing once I walked through my full reasoning. The ideas evolved through additional group discussions, and from suggestions emerging there, the Greenville Chamber launched a new economic initiative they titled Accelerate! Greenville.

As the objectives of the initiative began to take shape, the chamber initiated the process of finding someone to chair this new program. It was through other business dealings and through the chamber that I had come to know Craig Brown, who was the former president and chief operating officer of the Bcom3 Group, then the fourth largest advertising agency in the world. In 2006, Craig bought a minor league baseball team affiliate of the Boston Red Sox. He moved them from

Columbia, South Carolina, to Greenville and built a new stadium, and the Greenville Drive became an overnight hit in Upstate South Carolina. Craig and I became fast friends immediately, and we shared a dry sense of humor that we employed with regularity. When chamber leadership approached me to chair Accelerate! Greenville, my response was that the only way I would do it was if I shared the position with Craig. Ironically, the Chamber had approached Craig as well, and he had given them the exact same answer. We ended up cochairing the initiative for eleven years.

One of the first things we did was to catalog all the existing economic development entities that operated across the state of South Carolina. We were shocked by how many existed in the ten-county Upstate South Carolina area and across South Carolina as a whole. All were doing good, important work. Each entity took pride in what they were doing. There was a great deal of impressive activity being undertaken, but each was doing their own thing. A significant portion of our efforts overlapped, resulting in duplicative programs and numerous redundancies. Craig and I quickly recognized a pressing need for a unified plan to improve the coordination among the various economic development entities. In order to maximize the impact of the dollars and energy being invested by all the stakeholders, someone needed to find a way to get some or all of the key players to work together in a well-coordinated, integrated fashion.

We knew that getting the primary economic development organizations with strong boards and dynamic leaders to agree to work together would be challenging. It was a classic example of needing to know how to step on people's toes without taking the shine off of their shoes. We called a meeting and gathered everyone into the same room at the Greenville Chamber. In a direct but diplomatic manner, we reviewed the realities of Greenville's economic health and the challenge Greenville's minorities and underserved faced relative to economic mobility—the ability to improve their economic standing and quality of life. Much of what we were experiencing could be rectified more quickly if we worked together rather than independently. I shared with the group a simple concept that I called the four Cs of teamwork:

- Communication

- Cooperation

- Collaboration

- Coordination

All of these words represent action-oriented traits every organization needs to exhibit in order to function in an integrated fashion and at an optimum level of performance. When any one of these elements is missing, the result is a disjointed organization or an inefficient effort. Companies that have not mastered these four Cs are unable to move forward in lockstep with each other. And if you can't move forward together, many times you end up not moving forward at all.

Just as Craig and I did in the meeting we conducted with the various economic development entities, the process of majoring in the four Cs of Teamwork starts with listening. True *communication* begins with at least two parties who are speaking *with* each other, not to each other. Everyone deserves the opportunity to be respectfully heard. We welcomed diverse ideas and opinions in a manner where all involved

THE FOUR Cs OF TEAMWORK:

- Communication
- Cooperation
- Collaboration
- Coordination

felt heard and respected. Such an approach fostered an environment that enabled progress to be achieved through actions that represented the *collective* perspectives of the entire group. We created open communication channels that were never about establishing winners and losers, and we established a team and a plan for moving forward.

If you cannot communicate, then you will never be able to *cooperate*. The test of a truly great negotiation is that neither party gets exactly what it wants. And as long as you're not giving up something that is essential to your core beliefs—for me that is faith, family, and friendship—then the spirit of cooperation is always about finding a solution that can be accepted by all parties. No one is going to get everything they want, but we must find the middle ground where we can live and breathe and work together. With Accelerate! Greenville, we approached all the parties involved with open communication aimed at finding a way to work together with a purview toward becoming more effective and efficient. Our goal was to make sure the initiative revolved around a single unified economic development plan for the greater Greenville area.

> If you can't move forward together, many times you end up not moving forward at all.

Through cooperation, we were then able to *collaborate*, working together to identify who did what best. Just like in any partner relationship, each participant brings different assets to the table. By analyzing when different entities were developing programs focused on the same constituents or had mission overlap, we found ways to either join forces or help one entity redefine its focus. The goal became to take the same number of resources that were currently being diluted across four dozen different strategies housed in myriad organizations and create a channeled, targeted approach that could then reach critical mass. By *coordinating* our approaches and building off existing organizational strengths, we created a multiplier effect that accelerated the impact on the communities and constituents we were committed to serve.

What our little coalition of community economic groups realized as we came together to act on the mission of Accelerate! Greenville was the same thing every organization must learn: based on situational needs, resources and assets, expertise, and other factors, there are times when it is appropriate for entities to step up and take the lead, times where they need to be important collaborative partners, times when their role is to participate by following, and other times when they should step aside.

Indeed, there are times when it is appropriate to talk about a fifth *C*: consolidation. Whether it is with external partners coming together for the common good or teams within an organization working together to increase efficiencies, sometimes we discover that two or more individuals or entities are working on the same challenge or opportunity, but they are oblivious to each other's efforts. In these cases, the mission is usually better served with greater focus. That is when consolidation offers an appropriate alternative. Consolidation many times enables 1 + 1 to equal 3.2, not 2. It's ultimately about finding the most efficient way to achieve the desired results.

> You are going to achieve your collective goal faster if you pursue it in a coordinated fashion.

You can keep people mission-focused when you create a four Cs culture where everyone wholeheartedly acknowledges that the mission is to achieve the desired result or objective, even if it means one party has to take a back seat. When that happens, rather than stick your lip out and pout, I try to remember Roger Neely's astute advice, "Get better, not bitter." The immutable truth is that you are going to achieve your collective goal faster if you pursue it in a coordinated fashion. I will get into more detail on each of the four Cs as we look at achieving organizational and operational excellence in later sections. But first I want to explore some of the mantras that will help you achieve leadership excellence, which starts by understanding that it's one thing to be a great leader; it's another thing to be a great leader on a great team.

PART 2

LEADERSHIP EXCELLENCE: LEAD FROM THE MIDDLE

MANTRAS FOR EXCELLENCE:

O   Everybody from the janitor to the king deserves to be treated well.

O   The authentic leader embraces inclusivity and eschews exclusivity.

O   The authentic leader is collaborative but stops short of being democratic.

O   The authentic leader humbly accepts the word no from any level within the organization as long as that no is backed by sound logic or a proposed alternative course of action that fulfills a higher priority.

O   Praise publicly; correct privately.

O   You can do the *right thing* in the *wrong way* or at the *wrong time*, and the result can be worse than if you did nothing at all.

Chapter 12

EVERYBODY FROM THE JANITOR TO THE KING DESERVES TO BE TREATED WELL

Sometime in the late 1980s or early 1990s, I was teaching a twelfth grade Sunday school class at Taylors First Baptist Church in Taylors, South Carolina. This was in an era before most of us had printers at home, and I had failed to print out the handouts for my lesson before I left work that previous Friday. Because of that omission, I needed to drive to my office in downtown Greenville early on a Sunday morning to use the printer there to produce the handouts I needed. I printed the handouts, and as I was driving home, an old man in an even older car had broken down smack dab in the middle of the intersection of Park and Stone Avenues. This was not just in an age before most of us had printers at home; it was long before we had cell phones as well. I was running late. I still had to get home, pick up my family, and drive the ten minutes to church before I taught. Looking at my watch,

I drove through the intersection past the old man and the disabled car. I traveled another quarter mile or so and then a voice inside my head said, "This isn't right; I can't not help this guy. How can I place more importance on going to church rather than being the church?" I turned around. I went back and helped the old man push his rust bucket of a car into the parking lot of a local meat & three restaurant on Stone Avenue. I asked the man what help he needed, and he asked if I could take him home. I told him I would but that I had to make a phone call first. I can't remember if I went back to my office or to a pay phone, but I called Susan and asked her to call the eleventh grade teacher and ask him to cover for me. "I'm not going to make it to class," I said. She asked what had happened, and I told her I needed to help this man.

In that moment I realized that sometimes we're so focused on what it is we *think* is important that we miss what really is important—to help make the lives of those we encounter better. Out of that simple experience, I began to realize how often most of us pass by people in challenging situations and view them as interruptions in our day, interferences that keep us from our work or that allow us to fall into the belief that because of our station in life, we are better than others. Resisting such temptation that we all face in the hurried lives that we live, I composed a phrase that I have used for years to remind me of the importance of others: everyone from the janitor to the king deserves to be treated well.

As I have grown older, I have become acutely aware of my humanity and mortality. It's ironic, since death is the most inevitable thing about life, but we all live like we're immortal. Regardless, realizing the finiteness of life and my relative unimportance when compared to the reach of time and humanity, whoever I am and whatever I do—let's face it, I'm just not that important. This philosophy is nothing more than an extension of what I have stated earlier about humility. I don't know how or why, but I have never left the office after a long but successful day at work and felt like, "Man, I hit a home run today!" Maybe that's emotionally unhealthy, but that's how I feel. Whether it was how I was raised or what I have learned along the way, I am compelled to give more credence and credit to the team than to gloat over my own efforts or results. That attitude prompts me to try to give everyone a chance and to treat everyone well. But we have to be authentic in caring about others from all walks of life and not to do so for show or to fulfill our social obligations. This philosophy extends into leadership roles in a work environment. There's an old saying fathers tell their daughters when they are of dating age: "Watch how your boyfriend treats his mother because that is how he is going to treat his wife." When I am evaluating managers, I apply something similar, for I am not that interested in how those managers treat the leaders to whom they report; I am more interested in how they treat those who work for them. Do they serve their team members? Do they encourage and develop them? Do they invest in them?

Walt Bettinger, the CEO of Charles Schwab, takes this idea a step farther still. When he is reaching the decision stage of a potential hire, he invites the job candidate to breakfast—but he arrives at the restaurant early, pulls the manager aside, and says, "I want you to mess up the order of the person who's going to be joining me. It'll be okay, and I'll give a good tip, but mess up their order." Bettinger takes this unusual action because he wants to see how the candidate responds. Does the person get upset? Do they show their frustration? Or are they understanding? Observing them, he believes, helps him understand how they deal with adversity and provides insight into their core nature. As a simple situation offers "another way to get a look inside their heart rather than their head."[4]

How Bettinger developed such an unusual test for potential employees came from his own college experience through a test of another sort. Bettinger had maintained a 4.0 average all the way through college and wanted to graduate with a perfect GPA, but he then encountered a final exam in a business strategy course his senior year that threw him for a loop. He had felt fully ready and had studied for hours, confident he could apply memorized formulas. When the teacher handed out the exam, it was a single piece of paper. The side of the exam facing up was blank, and when students were instructed to turn it over, the back was blank as well. The professor said, "I've taught you everything I can teach you about business in the last ten weeks, but the most important message, the most important question, is this: What's the name of the lady who cleans this building?" Bettinger had no idea. It was the only test Bettinger ever failed. He said it made a powerful impact on him and that he deserved the B he received. Bettinger recalls, "Her name was Dottie, and I didn't know Dottie. I'd seen her, but I'd never taken the time to ask her name. I've tried to know every Dottie I've worked with ever since."[5]

It's a powerful lesson and a humbling one. I have tried to make sure I know the Dotties in my life. Don't pay any attention to the zip codes where people live, the cars they drive, or the jobs they hold. Those are not the measure of a person. Treat all with genuine kindness

---

4   Jacquelyn Smith, "Charles Schwab's CEO Takes Job Candidates to Breakfast and Asks the Restaurant to Mess Up Their Order—Here's Why," *Business Insider*, February 18, 2016, https://www.businessinsider.com/charles-schwab-ceo-takes-job-candidates-to-breakfast-messes-up-their-order-2016-2.

5   Jacquelyn Smith, "The CEO of Charles Schwab Learned the Biggest Lesson of His Career from Failing a One-Question Exam in College," *Business Insider*, February 9, 2016, https://www.businessinsider.com/charles-schwab-ceo-learned-biggest-lesson-of-career-after-failing-a-test-2016-2.

and respect. You never know where the best advice will come from or who will teach you the most important lessons.

I have taken Walt Bettinger's hiring approach to heart in a very literal fashion. I try to take everybody at the companies I have led out for lunch or breakfast, irrespective of position, and just get to know them. I don't talk business. I don't have an agenda. I just want to understand more about some of their innate talents and to learn about their interests. I am curious about what they want to become. I don't want to sell my team members; I want to know them. Making this a uniform practice across the company—from janitors to kings—I can fulfill at least two powerful principles I hold. The first is something I will devote a chapter to later, which is my belief that those people in our organizations who have the greatest amount of direct access to our prospects, customers, the market, and our work processes can offer the most accurate feedback about and insights into our performance, and they provide the best recommendations for improvement. The second is an important mantra for excellence: The authentic leader embraces inclusivity and eschews exclusivity. We're all in this together. Every person in our organization plays an important role in helping us fulfill our purpose, achieve our vision, and accomplish our mission. So let's behave like we like each other—like a team.

> Treat all with genuine kindness and respect. You never know where the best advice will come from or who will teach you the most important lessons.

Frankly, when I invest time in these relationships and come to know people as individuals, not only do I value them more because I know something about their lives, but together we create a more natural and authentic collaborative spirit in the organization. At the end of the day,

119

I am responsible for many of our company's decisions, but I want input from all who have relevant contributions to help inform the decisions I must make. The authentic leader is collaborative but stops short of being democratic. You can't make every decision based on the consensus of the group. Believe it or not, the majority is not always right. And when consensus can't be reached, you don't bring the decision down to a vote. The role of an authentic leader is to bring clarity to a cloudy situation or a murky set of choices. As Patrick Lencioni shared in his book *The Five Temptations of a CEO*, CEOs have to choose clarity over certainty. There are not many things in life or in business about which we are certain. We have all heard that the only certainties in life are death and taxes. Authentic leaders make decisions, and the decisions they make have to be clear. I may not be *certain* about the decision, but I have to be unwavering and clear in declaring, "We are going to take that hill!" Leaders have to own the decisions we make. My job as CEO is to represent the interests of the entire company, and that includes our employees, our customers, our partners, and our community. I welcome input that informs me in ways that help me make better decisions, but the buck stops there. It is my decision, and I have to own it.

Knowing the people I work alongside helps me see that every individual and every role within the organization has value, and that in turn allows me know to whom I can turn when I need data, information, and honest and insightful perspective. If I've done my part in helping shape the optimal culture for achieving excellence, we are a body of people where team members are not afraid to say no when they know it's in the best interests of the organization to avoid a particular direction or opportunity. The authentic leader humbly accepts the word *no* from any level within the organization as long as that no is backed by sound logic or a proposed alternative course of action that fulfills a higher priority.

Knowing our people as individuals also helps me assess when a team member might not be serving the organization to their fullest potential simply because they are not in a role that is well matched to their strengths. That is an entirely different scenario from a team member who is not pulling their weight. We want to position people for success. Don't saddle someone in your organization with a job that runs counter to their innate talents and doesn't mesh with their passions, interests, and inclinations as to who and what they want to become as a professional. We want people to grow into new responsibilities, to challenge themselves and tackle things they didn't know they could do, but I'm not going to take one of my most productive creatives and move them to accounting. What I do demand is that every team member strives for personal and professional excellence. We want the A team that produces A-level performance, whether that is fielding customer calls, helping develop our strategic plan, or cleaning our offices. As John Wooden said, the standard of performance is "your personal best." That is different for everyone, and our job is to help everyone achieve their personal best.

If I have a team member who appears to be in the right role but isn't rising to that A-level performance, or if they've made some decisions or taken some actions that have not landed well, I follow a simple but critically important mantra: Praise publicly; correct privately. I let the dust settle, then pull them aside alone, preferably in a neutral location, and then we discuss the situation diplomatically. Even if I am 99.99 percent sure that I know *exactly* what happened, I try to never start these discussions with an accusation. Instead, I start with a question: "What happened?" Although I am fully aware that I am on the receiving end of a single version of "the truth," I still almost always discover that the *known* facts are usually not *all* the facts. The purpose of this exercise is not to overtly punish or castigate the individuals for a mistake made in what is now the past but instead to teach and instruct to improve the future. Conversely, when team members have delivered work that exceeds the standard for excellence, or better yet, establishes a new standard, we want to make sure we acknowledge it. Acknowledgment and recognition don't have to take the form of loud displays or silly generic awards; instead, we can make it personal and write them a note, give them a small but unexpected cash bonus, or take them and their significant other to dinner. My experience is that team members remember the frequency of recognition and generosity more and longer than they remember the amount. And yes, if the performance is truly exemplary, we

> **When you value and encourage people, you always gain more than you lose.**

probably embarrass them a little bit with some public recognition. It's all worth it, because the truth is, when it comes to culture, it's all about people.

Think about how you wish to be treated by others. Don't we all want to be treated with respect? *Be human!* In those rare instances when showing kindness to others gets you burned or allows someone to take advantage of you, it's okay. Let it go. When you value and encourage people, you always gain more than you lose. And when you value people, they learn to value one another, creating a camaraderie that all can draw upon when facing demanding workloads or difficult circumstances.

MANTRAS FOR EXCELLENCE:

O Authentic leadership is always preceded by authentic living.

O Don't overstate your position, overplay your hand, or overstay your welcome.

O You get what you tolerate.

O Talk less; do more.

O Intrinsic security trumps external validation.

O "Activity without achievement is worthless." —John Wooden

O The numbers don't tell the whole story, but the numbers don't lie.

O In God we trust. All others, bring data!

O If you shortcut the process, you will probably short-circuit the results.

O Those who generate the returns deserve to share in the rewards.

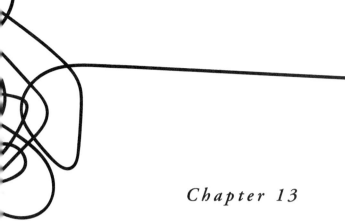

Chapter 13

AUTHENTIC LEADERS MEASURE RESULTS, NOT STYLE

Before I can talk about the results authentic leaders can achieve, I had better establish exactly what I mean by an authentic leader. I cannot take credit for this perspective, but I heard it once, and it has stuck with me that authentic leadership is always preceded by authentic living.

Authentic living starts with having integrity, which is simply doing what we say we are going to do. Authentic leaders don't make false promises. They follow through on commitments. It's somewhat humorous, but I have told those around me for years, "I'm going to do what I tell you I am going to do, but I might be late." It is easy to overcommit, and that may be one of my most glaring weaknesses. Being late is an area of underperformance on which I am constantly working.

Leadership starts first with who you are, not with what you do. If you are arrogant or superficial,

> Authentic leaders don't make false promises. They follow through on commitments.

others will see through you. All of us have our own innate and unique personalities, experiences, and leadership styles. Be true to yourself and true to your roots. Don't fake it. I'm not going to pretend to be something or someone I'm not, but I am always going to strive to be *better*. Sometimes I think I have been cursed by carrying the title of president or CEO, as those around me with whom I work for the first time generally formulate some instant opinions as to what is important to me and the kind of person I am. I tell everybody, and hopefully I live up to this, "I'm not going to surprise you. If I violate that commitment, then I screwed up. Our working relationship isn't a one-way street; we are mutually accountable to each other." I try to live by my belief that position, pedigree, and privilege mean nothing; performance means everything. Most professionals climbing the ladder think they've arrived if they get a reserved parking place in front of the building with their title posted on a sign marking it. Don't buy into that philosophy. Don't have an elevated view of yourself or overstate your station in life. Don't be presumptive or assumptive. I tried to come up with a memorable way to remind myself of this, as well as communicate it to others in my life, and it came to me one day out of the blue: Don't overstate your position, overplay your hand, or overstay your welcome. Those three directives are some of the best that I know to remind me to put others first, exhibit genuine humility, and behave with a degree of style, manners, and grace. Recognizing the impact of the little things that we do, and the cognizance that I don't get as much exercise as I used to (and really need these days!), I've made it a practice since 2006 when I became president of a company for the first time to park in the farthest parking place from the entrance to our building. And unless I am accompanied by a guest who reasonably expects that we will use the elevator to ascend to our third-story location, I take the stairs. Are some of those practices for my own health and fitness? Yes. But they are also subtle reminders to leave plenty of room for others to enjoy the rewards of life and business and for me to quietly excuse myself so that others can have center stage. The sun is a big old ball of light; make sure you let others stand in the brightest spot sometimes.

Ultimately, our integrity will always be measured by others through our actions, not our words. George Eliot said, "Our deeds determine us, as much as we determine our deeds." A somewhat cynical counterpoint to this idea that all parents know when it comes to children and all business leaders know when it comes to company performance is that you get what you tolerate. Which, of course, means the opposite is true as well. Integrity is ensuring that what we say we are going to do is consistent with our core ideology. What we commit to needs to be consistent with what we believe and what we expect from ourselves and from those with whom we choose to affiliate. We should make no false promises, and we shouldn't behave in a way that is incongruous with who we are and who we believe we should be. Not to be liked. Not to fit in. Not to pledge something we cannot deliver. Any incongruities between what we say we are going to do—or what we actually do—and our core ideology is the perfect definition of hypocrisy. John Maxwell reminds us that "power really is a test of character. In the hands of a person of integrity, it is of tremendous benefit; in the hands of a tyrant, it causes terrible destruction."[6] All these are reasons that one of the mantras I repeat most frequently is this: Talk less; do more. As I stated earlier and will reinforce here, performance means everything.

I only have six rules (a lot of principles and guidelines but only six rules) for operating a business. I believe that authentic leaders in

---

6   John C. Maxwell, *Real Leadership: The 101 Collection,* (Harper Collins Leadership, 2006).

some shape, form, or fashion exhibit and promote the first two in a consistent manner. First, we conduct our lives and business in a way that is legal, moral, and ethical, and we stay away from anything that even hints at being otherwise. We make that decision once, today, and even if someone offers us a billion-dollar opportunity, if it in any way borders on being illegal, immoral, or unethical, the answer is no. Second, we behave in a way both at work and away from work that reflects and reinforces our personal and company values and culture. It fosters trust in us by those with whom we come in contact, and when those individuals need the types of products and services that our companies sell and deliver, it makes it easy for them to transfer that trust to the organization that each one of us represents. Beyond those imperatives, all guardrails for achieving results are off. I think the origins of this phrase are ancient, but I always associate it with a wonderful Greenville attorney and community leader, Merl Code: "If you're going to lead the orchestra, you have to be willing to turn your back on the crowd." Have some conviction about who you are and the choices you make. Don't be a person who always must align yourself with the majority in order to feel accepted or be significant. Intrinsic security trumps external validation. Many people spend their entire lives trying to fit in and be like everybody else, when the real need of leadership is to figure out how you leverage your uniqueness. Don't try to be who you're not; instead, leverage who you are.

Within the bounds of behavior described in the immediately preceding paragraph, it is outcomes and output we must measure. Not likability and not the ability to appeal to the masses. As the legendary UCLA coach John Wooden said, "Activity without achievement is worthless." How do you measure the outcomes of your work? You will recall that I talked about participating in the beginnings of Accelerate! Greenville's private sector-fueled economic development initiative. As those involved studied Greenville's economic health and began planning for a more expansive future, we realized that we were all guilty of a bit of myopia. We knew Greenville so well that sometimes we saw only what was within our line of sight. We knew we needed objective data, so we set about securing it from a number of sources, including expert databases, what we could distill from our own businesses and municipal records, and from predictive trend data. Of course, all of us in business talk a great deal about data-driven decisions. It doesn't start and stop there, however. As a group, we understood that there is an important marriage between accumulating such hard data and the experiences of those on the ground doing the work. We had gathered a lot of collective local wisdom, and we weren't going to disregard that, yet at the same time, we understood that we needed the objectivity that data could provide. It is another application of data-informed intuition. There's a phrase I've used with regularity in every business I have ever run: The numbers don't tell the whole story, but the numbers don't lie. We're going to pay attention to all the things that make us human, but we will align that knowledge with math, science, data, and systems to make sure that we're making an informed decision. I think of this as triangulation. It is this sort of balanced decision-making that improves the quality and outcomes of decisions. It is how you achieve exemplary results. An easy way to remember the importance of leveraging objective, reliable information is another mantra: In God we trust. All others, bring data!

Once you have reached a decision, you need to establish and execute clear-cut approaches to activate those decisions. Without this systematic approach and sense of urgency, you end up making good on Coach Wooden's warning and generate a lot of activity without achieving anything of value. Wasted activity is wasted time. And wasted time is wasted money. Not only do business processes with performance metrics help you pinpoint inefficiencies before they become crises, but templated, streamlined processes enable you to produce consistent results—and scale. It is virtually impossible to grow and scale without some degree of standardization. The best processes need to be replicable and repeatable. In order to develop standard processes that are replicable and repeatable, they must be documented, which in turn makes them easier to improve, because you have a definitive artifact to which you can return and revise. Process creation, testing, documentation, and continuous refinement and improvement are hard. But you must do it. Because if you don't, you will have to live with the negative consequences. If you shortcut the process, you will probably short-circuit the results.

Streamlined, efficient processes may not be sexy, but that's the point. You generally don't get rewarded when you are engineering and documenting processes that help ensure the attainment of the desired results, no more than data can reveal panache. We're not evaluating gymnastic routines based only upon style and difficulty; the gymnast has to stick the landing too. It's all about the end result. That's when the rewards flow.

Simply stated, those who generate the returns deserve to share in the rewards. Your customers want products and services that perform exactly as they expect, and your owners and shareholders want measurable results that put dollars in their pockets. That being the case, the true test of an authentic leader is whether they deliver the desired results on a consistent basis. No matter how charismatic you are as an individual, you can't talk or hype your way to authentic

> **The true test of an authentic leader is whether they deliver the desired results on a consistent basis.**

leadership; you have to earn it by generating results. In order to achieve meaningful results, you need everyone rowing in the same direction, and there's one sure-fire way to accomplish this, which is what we will discuss next.

MANTRAS FOR EXCELLENCE:

- "If you want to go fast, go alone. If you want to go far, go together." —African proverb

- All long-term relationships, personal or business, require two fundamental ingredients: trust and respect.

- Organizational charts may give you a position, but only people can grant you power.

- You can't mandate genuine followership; you have to earn it.

- It doesn't matter if you're right or if I'm right. Let's just get it right.

- All meaningful and lasting change starts first on the inside and works its way out.

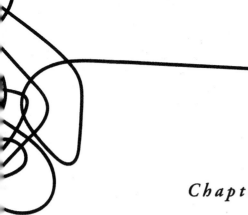

Chapter 14

AN ORGANIZATIONAL CHART MAY GIVE YOU A POSITION, BUT ONLY PEOPLE CAN GRANT YOU POWER

If you want to go fast, go alone. If you want to go far, go together. This proverb, whatever its true origin, has been uttered with frequency by a lot of people. That it is used often does not diminish its power or its accuracy. Most of the world's greatest achievements required more than a single individual to get the job done. It took a team. The best companies don't just use the phrase *team members* to refer to those who work there; they truly form teams that are united by common objectives that guide their actions.

Great organizational cultures produce great leaders at all levels. There are a lot of cliches regarding teams that emerge from sports—you've heard dozens of them—but they hold true both inside and outside sports. Consider the most common of these cliches: There's no "I" in "team." In business, we get a lot closer to our objectives if everyone, leaders included, works together with a maniacal focus upon the objective at hand. In football, the quarterback may call the play in the huddle, but the play cannot be executed if the other ten players don't each perform their roles. Half the time, the quarterback's primary job is simply to hand the ball off. Teammates aren't going to put in the hard work of executing their roles if they don't believe in

Great organizational cultures produce great leaders at all levels.

their common objective and believe in one another. Allow me one more sports analogy: How often have you seen a professional sports franchise invest a ton of money in the "best" player at every position and still the team flounders because they can't find a way to work together? Having one or more iconic "superstars" on a sports team is no guarantee of success. In fact, many times, performance on those teams actually declines rather than improves. The same thing happens in business all the time. In the businesses I have helped lead, it is not about having a handful of superstars who overshadow everyone else. It is much more about making sure that the following is true:

- I want people who are *good* at what they do (each team member's role aligns with their talent).

- I want people who *like* what they do (if they don't like what they do, they won't do it for long).

- I want them to like doing it *together*.

Even in today's increasingly virtual commercial world, the third point is still the most important. While working in the technology firms where I spent much of my career, I found that relational factors generally trump the technical factors when it comes to achieving success. And because positive working relationships are at the core of success, our organizations will do well to remember this mantra: all long-term relationships, personal or business, require two fundamental ingredients: trust and respect.

How do we build teams that trust one another? It starts by overturning conventional wisdom about leadership. Those people in our organizations who have the greatest amount of direct access to our customers and to our work processes often are the source of the most revealing insights about our performance and the quality of our deliverables. They are, literally, the most important team members in a company. To put this philosophy to work for us, we start by *inverting* the organizational chart.

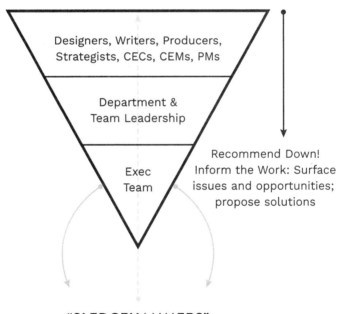

MARKET   PROSPECTS   CUSTOMERS   THE WORK

Designers, Writers, Producers, Strategists, CECs, CEMs, PMs

Department & Team Leadership

Exec Team

Recommend Down! Inform the Work: Surface issues and opportunities; propose solutions

"SLEDGEHAMMERS"
Serve up!
Eliminate obstacles and enable effective execution

At the top of an inverted organizational chart are those employees who work most directly with our customers and who are most responsible for delivering our products and services. Because they live it daily, they witness and experience firsthand situations to which those of us overseeing the overarching needs of the organization have limited visibility. We trust them to make recommendations based on their experiences and insights. Those throughout the management structure serve these employees and make certain they have the tools necessary to *delight* our customers and achieve our business objectives. I have worked in a number of industry verticals—manufacturing, material handling, apparel, information technology/software, and marketing—so while the specific jobs and roles held by those at the top of this inverted pyramid are different depending on the industries in which they work, their importance is not.

So what about those of us with the initials behind our titles? In traditional organizational structures, by placing the executive leaders at the top or in the center, what really occurs is that every critical decision that needs to be made across the organization arrives at their desks like this:

TYPICAL ENTREPRENEURIAL OPERATING MODEL

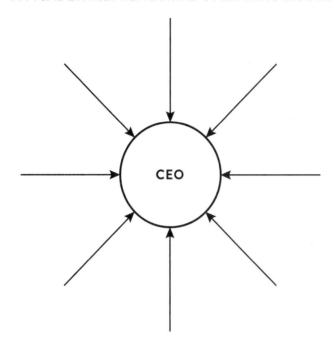

The problem isn't so much a lack of upward delegation through management levels charged with filtering out issues that don't need executives' attention as it is a flawed paradigm that directs all decisions of any magnitude to the C-suite. The prevailing culture is that the corner office must review and process all important information and ultimately make or explicitly bless all key decisions. In the long run, because the actual decision emanates from the C-suite, a false impression is created that all good ideas originate with or run through the executive team. This is a paradigm we must disassemble, because it discounts the thinking of our frontline workers and eventually marginalizes the primary source of an organization's most grounded and effective ideas.

By contrast, the executive team at the bottom of the inverted pyramid has one primary responsibility when serving those at the top: eliminating roadblocks. That's why we nicknamed executives sledgehammers. When a customer-facing team member or one who is responsible for executing one of our processes identifies a flawed process, a solution gap, a customer or market need, or any opportunity for improvement and alerts their manager, the manager is tasked with making certain that proper action is taken to equip and enable the process owner(s) to make the necessary changes to improve the current reality. If something internally or externally is impeding progress and success, it's an executive's job to break through or bust up (i.e., the sledgehammer metaphor) whatever is causing the roadblock, whether that's establishing contact with a hard-to-reach prospect, customer, or decision maker; authorizing a change to an ineffective internal process; securing needed technology; or whatever else will allow our subordinates to achieve their objectives. It is not the executive's job to complete a team member's objectives; however, it is the leader's responsibility to facilitate the removal of any impediments that are beyond the reach of our team member's expertise and experience to alleviate or disposition.

A team member's success is the organization's success. Our job is to help ensure that we are *all* successful. A leader's success is measured not by their *own* personal achievements but instead by what *others* do or become as a result of their influence. That's true power. Organizational charts may give you a position, but only people can grant you power.

With such a mindset, one that starts with an inverted organizational structure, meaningful collaboration will organically originate or accelerate. This is true because it is the best way to promote a genuine open dialogue and build trust. Our team members want to be consulted from the get-go and know that their ideas are being taken seriously and that any ideas that have merit will see the light of day. If we want broad engagement and buy-in from all corners of the organization, we have to recruit and involve team members at the ideation phase and not just at the implementation phase. At least since the deaths of John Kennedy, Martin Luther King Jr., Robert Kennedy, and other public figures assassinated in the 1960s, we have been living in an age when, with every generation, people's faith in authority has gradually eroded, whether that faith was in government, corporations, or individual leaders. The general public is skeptical about the truth and who is telling it. The workforce of today wants more control over their own destiny. They desire to provide meaningful input, and they want to participate in decision-making processes. And while the buck may stop with me because I am in a senior leadership position—which means the responsibility resides with me as well—we will be a stronger organization when we have more people at the table participating in the decision-making process. The number of good heads involved in the decision-making process usually improves the quality of the decisions made. Our titles may generate real or feigned respect from our employees, but you can't mandate genuine followership; you have to earn it.

Collaboration needs to start at the beginning of a project. We're better off assembling from day one a task force or speed squad to address a pressing challenge or opportunity in order to solicit a broad set of ideas and approaches to the issue we are trying to address. Yes, it is messier than making a unilateral decision. Theoretically, *their* way may take longer. Theoretically, *their* way may cost a little more. I don't care, because reality is different from theory. My experience is that this is many times the most effective—and cost-effective—approach to process or solution improvement. That's how we bring people on, how we get them engaged. Everybody buys in from the beginning rather than at the end. Team members won't as readily accept and adopt change that I unilaterally envisioned and designed as quickly and easily as they will adopt changes and improvements that they helped formulate. Authentic leaders are really experts at change management. They are adept at moving people from point A to point C in a such a subtle manner that when point C is attained, the journey was of such a nature that everyone looks around and asks, "How did we get here?" Because they were brought in as part of the solution envisioning process, the solution realization process was less bumpy and more efficient. The impact is a strengthened commitment to the organization's vision and increased trust in the leaders who believed in them.

Quite recently, I put this inverted governance structure and collaboration model to the test. Just three months into my tenure at Cargo, facing my first annual presentation on the state of the agency, I discovered that, as an organization, the company really hadn't formed a definitive vision or mission. Cargo had a clearly defined purpose—to make work and life better for our team members, our customers, and our community—but our vision, mission, and values were a little murky. I had my own version of those three organizational tenets that had played well in technology companies, but Cargo is a highly creative ad agency, a very different environment from most in which I had worked. Under a tight deadline and with little time available to solicit input, I decided to unilaterally promote a suite of slightly modified legacy vision, mission, and values statements in my first state of the agency meeting. All three landed with a thud. It was a good reminder for me that one size does not fit all. So I decided to take a different approach. First, I tasked our leadership group with talking to other team members to come up with a mission statement. Our creative director brought back a mission people really liked: "We create human success stories." It wasn't as hard-edged, finite, or measurable as the mission statements to which we had committed ourselves in my previous companies, but our people liked it. So I followed the approach that I espoused earlier: "Let's do it your way." "We create human success stories" became Cargo's official mission statement.

We'd gotten the ball rolling, but now we had to tackle our vision and core values. Over the years, I have been in literally hundreds of businesses that had their core values prominently displayed somewhere in their facility. Fortuitously, I had taken photographs of many of these core values and had them at my disposal. I went back through every core value I had gathered over my career, including those from my previous professional appointments, and compiled a three-page list of more than 120 core values candidates. I gave the list to the Cargo Culture Committee, which had four committee members at the time, and charged them with making a recommendation of three or four core values that our company could consider and adopt. The facilitator suggested that we needed additional participation on the Culture Committee to provide broader input to our core values and proposed expanding the committee to eight or nine members. I concurred. The expanded committee began to address the core values challenge. They came back with two they loved—"Love what you do" and "Create something great"—and a bunch of others around which they couldn't reach consensus. In my short experience at the company, one of the things I consistently noticed was that people tended to focus and expound upon problems rather than focus upon how those problems could be addressed or eliminated. It was a pet peeve about which I had been somewhat vocal, saying frequently that we didn't need people to illuminate problems; we needed people to solve them. As I looked through their list, I found a core value candidate that had tied for third place: "Be solution minded." I said, "That's perfect. Why don't we adopt that as our third core value?" The

Culture Committee agreed. I thought the values they had identified were crisp and tight, and most importantly, they'd come directly from the team. A couple of the Culture Committee members presented the proposed core values during one of our company-wide weekly Monday morning meetings, and all three were met with strong enthusiasm and unanimous endorsement. To me, this was an ideal example of true distributed leadership and evidence that the inverted leadership model can and does work.

Direction for this exercise did not come from the executive team; it came from our team members who now sit at the *top* of the inverted organizational chart. Yet we still needed a vision. Our current vision statement, while accurate—essentially about being the best B2B ad agency in the southeast—just wasn't very inspirational or synergistic with Cargo's creative heritage and staff. We needed a vision statement that answered this question: "What do we want to be famous for?" I told them that we were going to select two people from each of our departments—eight people total, with none coming from the leadership group—and form a visioneering team. Earlier in the year, I had secured an outside consultant, Tim Whitmire, to lead Cargo's objectives and key results (OKRs, for short) program development and deployment effort. Tim is the founder of CXN Advisory and cofounder of F3, the largest free men's fitness movement in the country. I asked Tim if he would be willing to facilitate Cargo's vision-setting process, and he accepted. Tim uses a metaphor that he calls the big tent philosophy that illustrates how an organization operates and how teams collaborate. Imagine a huge circus-style tent with a long center pole supporting the tallest part of the structure. The only way that center pole can stand is if numerous stakes are placed around the perimeter of the tent, each one equidistant from adjacent stakes in order to maintain equal tension on the center pole. Each stake represents a unique skill, a specific discipline, and, in many cases, a different perspective. Too much concentration in any one area (a stake) pulls the whole tent over in that direction. It's only through working together equally that the tent has stability. An organization without equally distributed diversity and perspectives among its teams and team members cannot stand. Applying this approach, Tim began to meet with our eight-member team and led them to formulate and articulate the future vision of the entire organization.

The principle that this approach represents is simple but profound: Everybody matters. We inverted the organizational chart and put our trust in our people so that they could put their trust in us. By using this intentional, equitable approach to engaging our team members in helping set company direction and strategy, including the definition of Cargo's mission, vision, and core values, we took a giant step forward in operating an organization that isn't afraid of taking calculated risks and doesn't care who gets the credit for being "right." One of my mantras is that it doesn't matter if you're right or if I'm right. Let's just get it right. This approach helps us draw the best out of everyone by allowing them to participate in those particular initiatives that play to their strengths. That's how you harness real power, for it recognizes that all meaningful and lasting change starts first on the inside and works its way out.

An organizational chart creates a framework for gathering input and ideas; a system of checks and balances to vet critical decisions; and the designation and delineation of resources dedicated to leading, serving, delighting, and growing customers. An inverted organizational chart recognizes that there is a difference between holding a position and being a leader. I place little stock in titles, but I watch what people do. True leaders *emerge*. Good executive leadership creates an environment that is the ideal balance of empowerment and accountability. Empowerment without accountability results in anarchy and chaos. But accountability without true empowerment or authority results in stasis—paralysis. Your future leaders will rise to the top in an environment that offers true empowerment with accountability—i.e., scorecard metrics against which performance can be gauged. The best leaders develop a consistent pattern of thinking—a framework for business reasoning—that results in a predictable pattern of behaviors and decision-making

Good executive leadership creates an environment that is the ideal balance of empowerment and accountability.

capable of transforming organizations and the people who work in them. This last piece of transformation—the ability to transform those around you—is one of the most vital aspects of leadership and can best be accomplished in organizations that invert power structures and distribute leadership opportunities to the very edges of the organization. The end game of such transformation is what we will look at next.

MANTRAS FOR EXCELLENCE:

O Leaders "hit 'em where they ain't." They go where others (the competition) aren't going or have not gone before.

O An option never considered was never really an option.

O Do less. Do it better.

Chapter 15

GREAT LEADERS LEARN
HOW TO THINK BEYOND

Most businesses, like most people, expend a great deal of time and energy looking backward. Maybe that's human nature, but we seem constantly to focus on fixing the last problem rather than anticipating the next one. We're reactive when we should be proactive. A better term to describe how we should act might be *anticipatory*. Take the Transportation Security Administration, for example. After September 11, airline passengers, rightfully so, could no longer carry onto planes sharp objects that could be weaponized. Next, after an incident raised fears about chemicals, we were limited relative to the volume of liquids we could carry aboard. Then, partially motivated by an incident in which a passenger was found with an explosive device in the heel of his shoe, we were asked to take off our shoes, whether we were a toddler, a grandmother, or someone with a known criminal record. I'm not minimizing the importance of air safety measures or suggesting that credible threats shouldn't be taken seriously no more than I'm suggesting businesses don't have to fix past problems, but some of the policies of the TSA are relatable examples of *reacting* or *responding* to incidents rather than *anticipating* potential threats by brainstorming in advance to identify and catalog the most likely types of threats and where related vulnerabilities and exposures exist that needed to be addressed. We face similar issues all the time in business. If we suffer a product failure or a service interruption, we expend a lot of after-the-fact focus and energy doing damage control to salvage the customer and our reputation when we probably should have invested the majority of that effort in advance to identify and anticipate likely scenarios and document and implement product or process improvements to head them off completely or establish standard contingency plans to effectively manage these situations should such a scenario occur.

Being anticipatory—looking ahead or thinking beyond today—is the best way to avoid future negative surprises. We're not perfect, and we're never going to be—more so if we are taking the risks that we *should* take to better prepare for the future rather than deal with the past—but how we learn from errors matters greatly, and they are lessons well learned if they help us avoid future missteps. As Peter Drucker said, "The best way to predict the future is to create it."

Sometimes we need to alter the patterns of how we think entirely. Sometimes we need to turn convention on its head. And always, we need to devote a healthy portion of our thinking time to determine what's next. Great leaders, and the great teams that they lead, think beyond the moment. They anticipate problems and challenges that might arise and head them off or prepare for them *before* they occur. Similarly, they see future opportunity where others aren't even looking. Leaders look for the white space, those emerging market opportunities that are not obvious to the naked eye and that most, if not all, of the other market contenders are ignoring. As Wee Willie Keeler, a Major League Baseball player for Baltimore and Brooklyn in the early twentieth century said, "Hit 'em where they ain't," *they* being the opposing fielders. Leaders "hit 'em where they ain't." They go where others (the competition) aren't going or have not gone before. They think into the future, and they think beyond what others have set as self-imposed boundaries.

As you might have guessed by now, I like to fish. You've probably also guessed that I don't get as much time to fish as I would like these days. When I do get the chance, I'm not primarily concerned with where the fish were yesterday, although I do consider that information. More importantly I want to figure out what has changed between

> Great leaders, and the great teams that they lead, think beyond the moment. They anticipate problems and challenges that might arise and head them off or prepare for them *before* they occur.

yesterday and today and *anticipate* what that means to the fish. Did a cold front that passed through cause the fish to move deeper? Did a high-pressure system and clear blue skies cause the fish to suspend and stop feeding? Was it a full moon last night under which the fish fed all night and have no interest in eating today? Or is a low-pressure system approaching that is going to trigger the fish to move shallow and feed more actively? I need to quickly assess the changes so that I can anticipate where the fish are going to be two hours from now when I am on the lake or in the Gulf. That doesn't mean I don't pay attention to historical patterns, places I've had success before, data on water temperature, barometric pressure, or the advice given by the best pro fishermen—that's the equivalent of the *historical* data that we gather and consider when making decisions for our businesses. Historical data is a key component in the decision-making equation.

However, I also have to take into account *predictive* data in order to best determine a future course of action. I look at the weather forecast for the next few days, the projected temperatures and cloud cover, rain chances and the resulting water color, rising or falling water levels, the tide schedules (if fishing salt water), etc. These are the data elements that I need to consider when deciding if I am going to fish, when I am going to fish, where I am going to fish, and what I am going to fish with. And when I am on the water, the best way that I know to catch fish is to try to think like a fish.

There's good advice in that metaphor. As business leaders, different types of decisions that we face dictate that we have to think like our customers, or our suppliers, or our partners, or our distributors. And we have to think like our team members or our shareholders, and yes, there are times when we need to think like our competitors. We can't train ourselves to *think beyond* if we can't wear a lot of different thinking caps. Smart leaders not only contemplate the present and the future from a myriad of different perspectives, but they consider and balance all of these various perspectives *concurrently*.

Such an ability is directly related to other characteristics that have to be part of the intelligent leader's toolbox. Intelligent leaders demonstrate three characteristics that separate them from the garden-variety leader or decision maker: (1) they can juggle a lot of things mentally (and physically) and keep all of them straight; (2) they can anticipate the consequences of their actions and the actions of those around them, not just to the first order of magnitude but to the second, third, or fourth order of magnitude; and (3) they have a penchant for and an ability to solve complex problems with multiple variables. The second characteristic is why people who play chess are good decision makers; they're thinking of the consequences—not relative to just the first move but what's likely to happen next and then what happens after that. Anticipating—looking ahead and thinking beyond—is a skill every leader *must* develop. And the best leaders not only are able to look ahead, but when a potential opportunity is just barely visible on the horizon, they exhibit a keen sense of judgment and discernment that enables them to differentiate between a lucrative trend and a passing fad. Trends carry the potential for longer-term ROI, but flash-in-the-pan fads will just take your money.

Like chess players, intelligent leaders visualize the next few moves and the consequences and opportunities that could result. They then weigh the options, not only anticipating the likely responses each move will precipitate from the competition but also the risk/reward factor inherent in those options. They consider *all* the likely scenarios as well as a few unlikely ones. They live by the mantra that an option unconsidered was never really an option.

There is what is typically referred to as a maturity model that represents how organizations tend to operate. At the lowest level of the scale are those people and organizations that *react* when something goes awry. We are caught flat-footed and make a quick decision to apply a not-yet-fully-developed solution to address what seems like an emergency or potential disaster. When we do that, we seldom think through all of the adjacent processes, people, departments, etc. that could be negatively affected. Often our reaction fixes the immediate problem but generates unanticipated consequences and causes collateral damage that results in new problems or trades one problem for another that is sometimes worse. Because it is human nature to react—the old fight-or-flight syndrome—we have to force ourselves to *slow down* (just a little) and consider the consequences of our options, following the idea of do less and do it better. Now, importantly, notice I said, "Slow down"; I didn't say, "Delay." I've already warned you of the inherent dangers in delaying a response.

Just take a breath, analyze what has occurred, catalog all of the valid options at your disposal, take the time needed to evaluate each option and its potential consequences, choose the best option based upon the facts at hand, then act on it. Don't panic and don't make a decision that is in effect a knee-jerk reaction. But don't become a victim of analysis paralysis either.

Sometimes rather than react, we *respond*. Being responsive sounds pretty positive, right? If we say we have highly responsive customer service, that sounds like something of which we should be proud. The problem is, when we are responsive or in response mode, someone other than us (usually a customer) beat us to the punch and identified a problem or an opportunity before we did, alerted us to it, and we are now responding to it. Being responsive is of a slightly higher order of maturity than being reactive but not by a lot. We may truly be responsive—and I certainly hope you are—when unexpected situations arise, for we want to demonstrate to our customers that they are our top priority, but the fact that our awareness of a problem or need arises only because someone external to the operation has pointed it out reveals that we are not systematically thinking ahead and thinking beyond. The emphasis that most businesses place on being responsive has prompted many organizations to provide twenty-four-hour phone access or the use of chatbots, which in many cases is necessary, especially for global organizations. After all, we do want to offer superior customer service because it can be a competitive advantage. The flaw in some (not all) of these services and practices, however, is that many of them have been put in place because the supplier of the product or service did not anticipate issues or questions in advance or provide a robust self-service portal that incorporates a knowledge base of all known and anticipated customer issues. When this is the case, the reality is that the business or supplier is still the second entity to know about a problem. If our customer discovered it before we did, is that really a best practice? We haven't done enough to anticipate their needs or the potential issues or questions or map out the evolving nature of their business. Responsiveness is not good enough.

Moreover, there should be a specific process in place for how we do respond when we fail to anticipate. It starts by making sure it is easy for your customer to tell you bad news. That means you must have a formal process of asking your customer how you're doing. We must listen from the top. Our customer-facing team members will be the ones who hear our customers' concerns, but if you follow an inverted organizational model, your leadership actively solicits feedback from those in direct contact with our customers and takes their input seriously. To honestly understand problems the customer has identified, we must be sincere in seeking their perspective and feedback (it's really the only one that matters) and invite them to tell us what we don't want to hear. When we properly address customer issues, the following progression occurs:

- Before problem arises: Customer *satisfied*

- Problem arises: Customer *less satisfied*

- Complaint handled well: Customer *more satisfied than before*

To achieve the "complaint handled well" stage in the previous progression can be an opportunity for creative brainstorming that leads to real process improvement breakthroughs that deliver a significant competitive advantage. Here's an example. There are few things people on either end of a transaction hate more than back orders. This distaste took on a whole different light during the supply chain shortages that occurred during the COVID-19 pandemic. Obviously, the real fix has to be one that gets to the *root* of the problem, which is to fix our broken supply chains and networks to improve availability, predictability, and reliability. But in the meantime, can you turn the problem into an opportunity that leads to customer satisfaction? Let's say you have a back order. Your customer complains. You're worried about your reputation. The product finally arrives, and you can fill the order. Your instinct is to get it out the door the second it is available. But what if instead of printing the packing slip and shipping label, you do one other thing first. You have a customer service representative (CSR) call that customer, apologize for the delay, inform the customer that the item in now in stock and available for shipment, and ask the customer if the item is still needed. If the item is still needed, the CSR should ask the customer if there are any other items the customer needs that could be shipped along with the back-ordered item to reduce the number of shipments and associated shipping charges. The customer leaves the exchange feeling more than satisfied, and if you're lucky, you just made an additional sale. I know this because I've helped lead businesses that have put such an approach into practice. It's a simple example of counterintuitive thinking. I've sometimes explained that the difference between react and respond is that responding takes a little more thought, a little more time, and sometimes a little more prayer!

Far better than needing to respond is to attain the highest level of maturity in the model: the ability to *anticipate*. We have looked ahead and seen what is, or could be, coming. To the best of our abilities, we have anticipated our customers' future needs. None of us are prophets or soothsayers, so all projections carry with them a margin of error to varying degrees. But any valid projection of possibilities or eventualities offers additional insights beyond what we can glean from only looking backward or just considering today. We need to be willing to burn the mental calories to understand shifting cultural, market, and economic trends and patterns that elevate our chances of identifying opportunities before others do. When we introduce a new idea, approach, or service, the response we are looking for is, "Wow, we would have never thought of that, but that is exactly what we need!"

Reacting is never ideal but occasionally unavoidable. Responding is better but not great, but it does bring into play our problem-solving abilities that, if highly developed, can actually turn a negative (a problem) into a positive (a happier customer than before). We would be wise to be innovative, inventive, and purposeful in how we go about examining those things that need fixing or improving. This is why approaches like the five whys can work, for by really digging in and repeatedly asking *why* a particular situation occurred or a specific problem arose within a team environment, you are open to a full exploration, and it allows you to identify the root problem. If you can't get to the root, you're only creating temporary patch-like fixes.

Anticipation is superior to reaction and response by an order of magnitude.

If there is a maturity level beyond the ability to anticipate, it is literally found within the word itself: *beyond*. Authentic leaders can accurately assess their customers, digest and assimilate the flow of current events and mindsets, understand workplace cultures as they evolve, and propose inventive, original ideas. They literally think differently and approach familiar subjects from a different viewpoint. Authentic leaders are not afraid to think counterintuitively; they don't start where the rest of the world is but rather they look at the other side of the coin. What if we started at the exact opposite perspective from where everyone else is and then mentally worked forward from there? Many times, the greatest advancements come from ideas that defy conventional wisdom and are completely out of bounds or off the chain. Most advancements and improvements are incremental, but every now and then, a real breakthrough results from an idea that in the beginning is roundly met with the response, "You must be crazy!"

An example that was vitally important to our business when I was the president of OOBE came about, as many ideas do, in the most unlikely of ways. We had a large client in the quick service restaurant industry that wanted to reinvigorate their team attire without completely revamping the entire uniform program, which would have taken a sizable investment. As I visited their facilities to learn about their history and their corporate culture, one thought occurred to me again and again—no team member, especially the teenager working their very first job, wants to be caught wearing a uniform that makes them look *exactly* like everyone else with whom they work. That thought nagged at me. How could we design a uniform that clearly identified someone as a representative of the company without having all employees dress identically? The solution we conceived came about in a very unconventional manner.

I have been fascinated—some would say obsessed—with Route 66 since I learned a little about its history in the 1990s. My wife, Susan, and I have driven its full length from Chicago to Santa Monica once and most of its length a second time. For me, Route 66 is a part of Americana that we need to find a way to preserve. I had long heard rumors that there is a fifteen-mile-long stretch of the original Route 66 near Miami, Oklahoma, that is only nine-feet wide. Legend has it that the state didn't have enough money to build two lanes, so they just built one. I don't know whether that is true, but what is true is that this part of Route 66 was routinely "buried" by the state to keep people from driving on it because it is only one lane and therefore not safe to drive. When the state covered up the roads, the local Route 66 "fans" would venture out at night and uncover it! I had read somewhere that if you went to a particular burger joint in Miami, Oklahoma and asked for a guy named Waylon, he could give you directions to this hidden section of Route 66. The rumors proved true, and although Waylon wondered just who was asking for him, he gave me directions on how to find this stretch of backcountry, single-lane strip of blacktop that runs from Miami to Narcissa.

This stretch of the original Route 66 is sometimes called the Ribbon Road or the Sidewalk Trail, appropriately so because of its unusual construction. They did not use rebar to reinforce the road; instead, they poured two inches of asphalt atop five inches of concrete that extends under the roadbed and forms six-inch-high curbs on both sides of the pavement. It is these curbs that provided the nine-foot-lane its strength and stability. Now what's this road got to do with uniforms, you ask? Well, it was while we were driving this unique stretch of historic highway that the business problem rumbling around in the back of my mind suddenly seemed to have a clear solution. I turned to my wife and said, "I've got it figured out."

"Figured what out?" Susan asked.

"How we retain a brand's identity while still giving people a sense of individuality." Susan gave me one of those I-love-you-but-you're-crazy looks. It was seeing those curbs in Miami, Oklahoma, that gave me the idea. I've come to reference it as the Curb model. The concept was simple. The bulk of the uniform investment was the roadbed. Most of the cost of the program would go into the core components of their attire, things like pants and shirts and hats; all those items would be available only in the brand standard colors. The smaller investment, the curbs, was in flair items such as ties and pins and other accessories that associates could pick and choose from to personalize their attire. The core elements of the uniform clearly represented the company, but the ability to personalize the uniform made the wearer feel like they were not simply a cog in a machine. Our client loved the idea, and it helped validate and make real OOBE's tag line at the time, "Uniforms that aren't."

You just never know where good ideas will come from. The curb model is confirmation that even when working within strict brand and product standards and guidelines, there is usually room to inject counterintuitive ideas that become game changers. Quantum leap ideas are hard to come by if you're not willing to stretch your thinking beyond the conventional and into the uncomfortable.

> Quantum leap ideas are hard to come by if you're not willing to stretch your thinking beyond the conventional and into the uncomfortable.

Of course, the freedom, desire, and drive to think ahead or postulate new patterns or trends will die on the vine if we don't build a culture that supports such creativity and that demands breaking with the way things have always been done. One of an authentic leader's important jobs is to teach others, and that test of leadership is where we go next.

MANTRAS FOR EXCELLENCE:

○ Your legacy of leadership will not be defined by what you did or achieved; your legacy of leadership will be recalled and remembered by others because of what they became, did, or achieved as a result of the relationship that you had with them and the positive influence that you exerted in their lives.

○ Authentic leaders aren't characterized by having a large office but instead a large following.

○ "Leaders eat last." —Simon Sinek

Chapter 16

THE TEST OF AUTHENTIC LEADERSHIP

The real test of authentic leadership—the only one that matters in the end—is this: Did I tell you something, show you something, give you something, or teach you something that you could easily put into practice and that, when you did, made your life, personally and/or professionally, better? I ended the last chapter talking about transformation, and this is the most important transformative effect a leader can have on the people around them. Whether you realize it or not, your legacy of leadership will not be defined by what you did or accomplished; your legacy of leadership will be recalled and remembered by others because of what *they* became, did, or achieved as a result of the relationship that you had with them and the positive influence that you exerted in their lives.

I can honestly say that I am most content when focusing on people and activities that reach beyond myself. I take great pleasure in watching someone discover that at which they are genuinely good or witness them take a risk by trying something they've never done before and flourish. Or fail, but stick with it, and then flourish. If we want to build companies that are the best in the world at what they do, where excellence is the true differentiator, then the way to do that is to fill them with the best people operating at their best. That's really what building a team is. It takes more than a great leader to be successful. And a leader is not a great leader or truly successful if they cannot transfer some of their knowledge, insight, and passion to others. Leaders are aggregators.

> **A leader is not a great leader or truly successful if they cannot transfer some of their knowledge, insight, and passion to others.**

We bring disparate people with disparate talents together. That is why authentic leaders aren't characterized by having a large office but instead a large following. A leader's performance must be measured by their ability to generate results through others. If the culture of the businesses we run encourages our people to strive to be their best, then the business has a chance to run at its best.

We all want to be known as being influential, but influence can be sporadic or situational. All of us have the opportunity to be a positive influence, but we can also be a bad influence if we are not careful. Positive influence, exerted consistently over an extended period of time, is leadership. Leadership is lasting but requires commitment. We don't really know when an action, comment, feedback, challenge, or compliment will initiate transformative change or inspire someone to a new level of performance, so we have to be consistent as leaders and true to ourselves and our values.

Finding satisfaction in the success of others within our sphere of influence is about genuinely wanting others to accomplish meaningful objectives and love what they do. Like all demanding but good things, it's a habit that must be developed. When Simon Sinek wrote the book *Leaders Eat Last*, it was more than an acknowledgement of humility; it represented an entire paradigm shift that inverted organizational structures and encouraged leaders to find satisfaction in other people's ability to thrive because it recognized that an essential element of real leadership is the willingness to place others' interests before your own.[7]

> If the culture of the businesses we run encourages our people to strive to be their best, then the business has a chance to run at its best.

This belief is one of the tests of authentic leadership. It is a belief that extends far beyond our businesses. I coined a phrase a few years ago that whatever job I held, it would be about the five Fs. It goes like this. A job needs to provide enough *financial* reward and *free* time (the first two Fs) to invest in the three Fs that are genuinely important: your *faith, family*, and *friendships*. If your job provides ample financial reward but no free time, then your job *is* your life, because you have no time for the other three Fs: faith, family, and friends. I have tried to ensure that who I am, the me I carry into the businesses I help lead, is aligned with this philosophy. I would be the first to admit that sometimes I fall short of my own standard. Today, primarily because of technology, most of us have become nonlinear workers. We no longer work from 9:00 a.m. to 5:00 p.m. as our parents or grandparents may have. The laptop computer, the tablet, and the smartphone have enabled us to work whenever, wherever. Windows of opportunity open and close on schedules that we do not dictate, and as leaders, it is our responsibility to capitalize on legitimate opportunities when they arise. So I sometimes find myself

---

7   Simon Sinek, *Leaders Eat Last*, (New York: Portfolio, 2014).

working at times normally reserved for spending time with family or others. However, I have to balance such times with others when I am off the grid so that over the long haul, I fulfill my commitment to invest in my faith and those people around me.

We think we are going to be most content when we have all the money in the bank that we will ever need, our 401(K) is flush, we live in the perfect house at the right address and we have no mortgage, we drive the car of our dreams, and we vacation wherever and whenever we want. It's not true. I find that when I concentrate on myself, I descend into thinking about what I want, what is not going the way I want it to, and who around me is not living up to my standard. However, when helping someone else find satisfaction, confidence, and excellence in themselves, you don't have much time left to think about yourself or what you don't have. I had to work through this for a number of years before I came to this position. It is counterintuitive to think that my contentment hinges on me helping someone else achieve *their* success and significance, but it has proven to be true time and time again. Help others, and by doing so, you help yourself.

PART 3

ORGANIZATIONAL EXCELLENCE: CULTURE TRUMPS STRATEGY

MANTRAS FOR EXCELLENCE:

O   We talk with each other, not about each other.

O   "Culture eats strategy every day for breakfast." —Peter
    Drucker

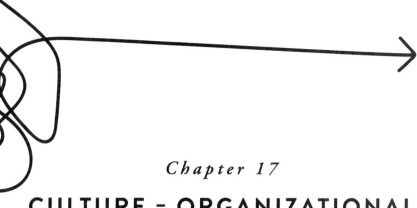

Chapter 17

CULTURE = ORGANIZATIONAL PERSONALITY[8]

So you want a positive, productive, everybody-gets-along, and out-come-focused culture in your business, right? A well-oiled machine. A place where people are knocking down the door to get hired. A business utopia. These are noble aims worth attempting. But let's start with a bit of reality: It ain't gonna happen. Or more precisely, it ain't gonna happen without a whole lot of work and commitment and not without installing the proper framework. What kind of organization do you want?

Should we aim for all those qualities I just listed? Of course. Might we get close? Yes, on our best days. But businesses are made up of people, and people have personalities and idiosyncrasies, and even the best people have bad days and unpredictable personalities. It takes intentionality, people-focused leadership, conscious and conscientious hiring, constant reinforcement, hard work, and more to develop and

---

8   Patrick Lencioni, *The Advantage: Why Organizational Health Trumps Everything Else in Business,* (San Francisco: Jossey-Bass, 2012).

maintain a business with a sustainable positive and productive culture. A culture is an amalgamation of a few important elements: a suite of intentionally architected, shared philosophies or approaches that connect individuals at a visceral level in a way that infuses communal philosophies and behavior patterns. Shared belief in those philosophies results in a consistent, predictable pattern of behavior demonstrated toward families, friends, and business associates. An organization's culture is essentially its personality. So think about the personality of the people with whom you most enjoy working and who help you perform at your best. What are those traits? How do we create an organization that shares those traits? Culture as an organizational personality is comprised of the following:

- Purpose: Why do we *exist*?

- Vision: What do we want to *become*?

- Mission: What do we want to *achieve*?

- Values: What character traits do we want to *embody*?

The process I detailed earlier about how a group of Cargo team members came together to define these company anchors was, at its root, addressing these questions.

A positive, productive, and cohesive culture is essential to optimum performance. Sadly, many of the traits indicative of the cultures we want embodied by our organizations run counter to some of the trends that we see in society and commerce today. Regardless, virtually all the leadership traits I have discussed thus far are the same kinds of traits we need to inculcate within the organizations we lead. They include the following:

- A culture of service. As team members in an organization, we serve our customers and one another. Their needs come first.

When we meet their needs with excellence, optimal performance follows. That means we treat one another as humans. My signature question—What can I do to help you?—becomes *the* question for everyone in the organization.

- A culture of encouragement. We don't beat people down; we lift them up. We correct in private, and we praise in public. We acknowledge excellence. We recognize people when they've done

> A positive, productive, and cohesive culture is essential to optimum performance.

well. We support one another when the demands are difficult. A culture of encouragement motivates teams to invent and take calculated risks, keep going when the going is tough, and exhibit greater thinking.

- A culture of empowerment. I'm going to ask a lot from you if we work together, but I'm going to make sure you have the authority and the resources to accomplish that with which you have been charged. I can't give you that power, but together we can help shape an organizational personality where you can seize it for yourself. You will have the authority to make decisions within your body of knowledge, domain of expertise, and span of control. We cannot have empowerment unless we are in the same boat, rowing in the same direction, because the boat is bigger than anyone on it, and the mission can be accomplished only when the boat arrives at its destination, on time and in one piece.

- A culture of accountability. In a culture of empowerment, you get to make decisions, and accompanied by a culture of accountability, you are responsible for those decisions. Authentic leadership is responsible for creating a work environment that is the ideal balance of empowerment and accountability.

- A culture of inclusivity. That boat—yeah, well, we're all in it together, and we all have important jobs to do to keep it moving in the right direction. Humility, teamwork, focus on objectives—these are all mechanisms by which we embrace inclusivity and reject exclusivity. No team member, wherever they happen to be positioned on the organizational chart, is any more important than any other team member.

- A culture of discipline. If our organizational culture is right, we're probably having a lot of fun doing the work we do, but we're disciplined in how we go about it. We give our best effort all the time. Discipline means having the intrinsic motivation to do the important things that need to get done, whether anybody knows about it or is pushing me to do so. It took me a while to learn to be disciplined, but once I did, it stuck, principally because I came to see the good that the organization could accomplish would be multiplied if we did what truly needed to be done rather than what we wanted to do. Sometimes those two are one and the same, but sometimes they are not.

- A culture of respect for all levels, roles, and individuals within the organization. From the janitor to the king. We affirm inclusivity by treating everyone with respect and dignity. That means we talk *with* each other, not *about* each other.

- A culture of innovation. If we're not ahead, we're behind. We do business in constantly changing environments. We must apply the four As—adapt, adopt, apply, adjust—and develop or modify new ways to address rapidly evolving marketplace requirements and new situations. As Roger Milliken said, "Operational excellence secures the present. Innovation excellence secures the future."

Organizations that embody these traits hold a significant competitive advantage because it enables them to attract, hire, and keep the best people. This reality is what led to the famous phrase usually attributed to Peter Drucker: "Culture eats strategy every day for breakfast."

To make these traits achievable, we must have the right people performing the right functions in ways that showcase their passions and strengths, and that's part of what we will look at next, which starts with hiring the right people in the first place and then making sure they serve in roles that align with their inclinations, interests, talents, and experience.

> We must have the right people performing the right functions in ways that showcase their passions and strengths.

MANTRAS FOR EXCELLENCE:

O "Hire green or hire great, but don't hire individuals in the middle. Those in the middle, for whatever reason, tend to stay in the middle." —David Pence

O The magnitude of the consequences or the cost is not a factor in determining whether something's right or wrong.

O Everybody's level of expectation and understanding is directly related to their prior degree of exposure.

O The mark of a truly intelligent person is that they can hold two diametrically opposed thoughts in their mind at the same time and give equal consideration to each.

O Passion precedes motivation.

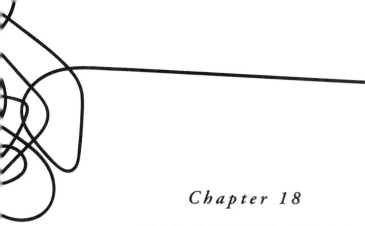

Chapter 18

THE SEVEN SEAS
(Cs) OF HIRING

What is business at its most basic? It is the act of *trading* goods and services. That idea—trading—has been with humans from the very beginning. "You're good at killing mammoths; I'm good at cooking meat. Let's make a deal." It could not have been long before some pre-historic genius thought, "I can teach others how to kill mammoths and not put myself at risk of being gored or trampled," and thus humans began hiring other humans. Some other genius thought, "Hey, they don't have any mammoths in that region, but they have great tubers; we should trade." A business was born. Trade routes were established, and employees did the dirty work. As trade extended across con-tinents, among several cultures in more ancient times, rather than label the five oceans, people referenced the seven seas when speaking about the world's major bodies of water along trade routes. But how did our mammoth dealer form the best teams that executed the best trades at the best prices with the fewest headaches? If I could have a conversation with this business ancestor, I'd draw on what I call the seven seas (seven Cs) of hiring.

When you're really good at hiring great people, everyone wants to work for you. At Cargo, for instance, even though we are a relatively small organization in terms of total team members, we receive multiple inquiries every day from people wanting to know if we are hiring. I've heard people around Greenville joke, "There's nobody left to hire in the marketing business in Greenville because you've hired them all!" We don't have a magic wand and pixie dust, we're not the pied piper, and we don't have to scour the seven seas to try to find talent, but we do have very specific traits we look for in our people. People are, after all, what make us successful.

> **When you're really good at hiring great people, everyone wants to work for you.**

If people are the key to building a successful organization, how do you hire the right ones? Well, for starters, they have to be people who fit our culture. So how do we find and hire individuals who embody our culture? We adhere to the seven seas (err, the seven Cs) of hiring:

- Competency
- Character
- Calling
- Contribution
- Commitment
- Collaborative
- Chemistry

Early in my professional career when I was still a bit green myself, I learned about the importance of three of these traits—competency, character, and chemistry—the hard way. Thinking I knew what I was doing when I first started hiring people, I put character in front of competency in my list of desired traits, and it got me in trouble. I knew I wanted to hire people of good repute and integrity, yet I failed to follow what Marcus Buckingham talks about in his book, *First, Break All the Rules*. Buckingham reminds us that we can transfer knowledge and teach skills, but we can't do anything about talent. I dutifully set about finding people who were hardworking and disciplined and who possessed the integrity to be honest and

THE SEVEN SEAS (SEVEN Cs) OF HIRING

- Competency
- Character
- Calling
- Contribution
- Commitment
- Collaborative
- Chemistry

forthright. And while I absolutely stand by the importance of these sorts of traits, the problem was that their talents and their competencies weren't aligned with the requirements of the jobs I needed them to perform in the roles I asked them to fill. In short, I hired good people, but they weren't competent people, at least not relative to the roles for which I hired them. The first lesson of hiring is that while we want to employ high-character people, we must make certain that our first filter is competency.

In an ideal world, we've got the budget that allows us to bring in a seasoned professional with a proven track record of success in the field for which they are being hired, someone with a proven mix of expertise and experience, what I dubbed E^2. Their expertise and experience have to align with the role for which they are being hired. If your budget allows you to hire someone experienced, and they also carry the quality of character and bring good chemistry to the team, not only will they grow the area of the business for which they are responsible but also they can become a kind of player/coach who can lead and grow their team and meld well with the rest of the organization. Character shows up the most not when things are going right for someone but when they are going wrong. Do they own their mistakes and are they able to say—and mean it—"It's my fault. Blame me"?

If we don't have the budget required to hire an E^2 candidate, then we need to look for the candidate with lots of raw talent who hasn't been developed. David Pence, the founder of Acumen IT in Greenville, shared with me when I was Acumen's president, "Hire green or hire great, but don't hire individuals in the middle. Those in the middle, for whatever reason, tend to stay in the middle." It's advice I follow to this day. When I don't have the budget to hire someone with a long history of being a top producer or a stellar performer, then I look for green (less experienced) professionals who meet the criteria of being hungry, humble, and smart, as Patrick Lencioni promotes in his book *The Ideal Team Player*. Over the years, I slightly modified Patrick's three criteria to better describe my vision of the ideal green candidate. Those three qualities are intelligence, initiative, and integrity (I^3). When hiring green individuals or professionals, we are more than willing to invest in their development when we know they possess those three qualities. Great or green, they either have a history of proven competency or they possess the I^3 qualities that will propel them toward competency at a rapid pace.

When we hire green, there will be competencies that are not developed or visible yet, which in turn means that, as these team members learn and take on new responsibilities, they will make mistakes. It's inevitable. As I have suggested, that's exactly when character is revealed. Do they accept responsibility? They live by the mantra that the magnitude of the consequences or the cost is not a factor in determining whether something's right or wrong. Do they avoid delay? Do they demonstrate integrity? That means living by the belief that what is right for the company, the customer, and the project is more important than being right. When such qualities of character are present, they will learn from their mistakes and move forward to develop the skills and capabilities they need to execute with excellence, make good decisions, and ultimately become effective leaders.

We need to create situations and scenarios during the interview process where we can honestly assess character, and we need to look at each individual's past experiences through a particular lens. For example, when candidates discuss why they are looking to leave their present position, do they talk about or blame others for the situation in which they find themselves? For me, that's an immediate red flag. My first rule for all of our team members is to be professional. What does that mean? For one, that means you don't talk *about* people. You talk *with* them. It takes a much bigger man or woman to talk with somebody than it does to talk about somebody. And they consider others' points of view without judgment. The world is a lot more of a complex and diverse place than any of us realize, and none of us have cornered the market on truth and fact. We are all a product of our upbringing and our experiences. Some of us have experienced more than others, and all of us have experiences that differ from those of others. In fact, one of my mantras is this: Everybody's level of expectation and understanding is directly related to their prior degree of exposure. An example would be food. If I had never eaten a steak in my life, I might be served what in reality was a not-very-tasty, somewhat tough cut of beef and think it was the best main course I had ever eaten. However, if I have traveled the world and eaten in some of its finest restaurants, I have developed a more sophisticated palate, and I can tell the difference between a wet-aged and dry-aged rib eye and how much marbling the cut of beef needs to maximize its taste without making the meat fatty. Because my expectations relative to food are educated and elevated, I might complain if the steak I ordered did not meet my expectations relative to cut, aging, and temperature. The point is this: We have to realize that everyone with whom we come in contact is at a different age and stage in life. It is incumbent upon us to share our experiences and knowledge with those who are eager to learn but to do so with an attitude of humility, patience, and grace. I know more only because I have been exposed to more; it is not because I am better than someone else.

Consistent with one of the qualities in our I^3 hiring criteria list, individuals of high intelligence can absorb, digest, and assimilate information quickly and then effectively and productively apply that information in short order. They also understand the importance of listening and considering others' points of view, even when markedly different from their own, as that is one important way that we expand our base of knowledge and learn. I heard it said once that the mark of a truly intelligent person is that they can hold two diametrically opposed thoughts in their mind at the same time and give equal consideration to each. Those are the sorts of minds I want working in our company.

I cannot speak about the character we seek in the people we hire without turning once more to John Wooden, the legendary UCLA men's basketball coach. I have been blessed in my life in a number of ways, but among them was the opportunity to hear John Wooden speak in person. He was ninety-six years old at the time, and the way he spoke in an interview style format before a large group of restaurant owner/operators about his life philosophies is something I will carry with me for the rest of my life and something that regularly reminds me of the kind of person I want to be. I also walked away from that encounter with Coach Wooden with something physical as well, a business card-size conveyance of wisdom that I have carried in my wallet ever since. It is dog-eared now from repeatedly extracting it from my wallet to refresh my memory as to what it says or to share it with someone with whom I am having a discussion on the topic of character. On one side of the card, it says the following:

TWO SETS OF 3s

Never lie,
never cheat,
never steal.

Don't whine,
don't complain,
don't make excuses.

On the other side is one of John Wooden's favorite poems, this one from the Reverend Henry van Dyke:

Four things a man must learn to do
if he would make his record true:
To think without confusion clearly,
To love his fellow man sincerely,
To act from honest motives purely,
To trust in God and Heaven securely.

When we have determined that a candidate is competent and is of good character, then we can try to assess how they will fit into the larger organization. Chemistry is the last qualification on our list of hiring criteria because it is the final filter that must be passed if one is to be invited to join our company in its mission. A candidate can meet the other six criteria with flying colors, but if they don't mesh with the rest of the organization, the resulting effect can be disastrous. Chemistry is sort of like baking; you need a number of unique ingredients all working together to bake a great cake. You have to find the balance of ingredients or you ruin the whole thing. Overdo the salt and no one is going to eat the cake. How you bring a very diverse set of capabilities and assets and experiences together into a business is what makes an enterprise that's truly unique and outstanding. A category of one kind of company. We're not looking for a herd of people who all think alike and love the same things, but they do have to respect one another's values and interests, be willing to subjugate their own personal objectives under a set of company objectives designed for the collective benefit of all employees and customers, like one another well enough to work amicably together, and then take pride and pleasure in seeing how each team member brings something distinct and positive to the group. The best test of chemistry in a business is when you hire a new team member, and although they've only been there two weeks, their integration into the company is so smooth and seamless that it feels like they have *always* been there. They've found a way to synergistically blend their competencies with the other strengths on the team. Diversity and chemistry should be fully symbiotic when it comes to the assembly and operation of any team. What makes us different should make us stronger—and better. Good chemistry is the big tent metaphor put into action, with the diversity each individual brings applying tension on that center tent pole in a balanced manner.

When a business has positive chemistry among its people, then each person can pursue and fulfill their calling. I have encountered so many people, especially less experienced professionals, who were opportunistic in how they secured their first or second job, and those positions just were not the ideal fit for their competencies, or they were not experiencing positive chemistry in the work environment in which they found themselves. Realizing this, but not truly understanding what was wrong or what to do about it, too often they run *from* something rather than run *to* something, wanting out of a situation without placing enough emphasis and importance on what they are looking for and what their real calling is. They haven't taken a systematic approach to identifying who they are, what they are good at, what they are passionate about, what they need to work on, and what they are looking for in a professional engagement that would enrich not just their careers and their bank accounts but also their lives. We need team members who have invested some thought in identifying three things: (1) what they are really good at, (2) what they genuinely love to do, and (3) what the marketplace will pay them well to do well. That's a person's dream job, right? To be paid to do what you're good at—and you love doing it! They have come to understand that passion precedes motivation. That realization will help them identify roles that are a better fit for them. Good leaders draw on that passion to motivate subordinates to achieve excellence.

> Diversity and chemistry should be fully symbiotic when it comes to the assembly and operation of any team. What makes us different should make us stronger—and better.

Individuals seeking their next professional appointment need to identify the types of organizations where they can thrive that fit their nature and needs. Large, small, local, national, global, closely held, public, centralized, decentralized, virtual, industry, etc. For the employer or leader, the intersection between what we need as a company and what a potential or new team member loves to do and what they are good at must be substantive, clearly evident, and expandable or the relationship will be short lived.

Businesses can thrive with team members who are in positions where they can pursue their calling, but we run businesses, not charities, and it is our jobs as leaders to put butts in the right seats so that they can leverage their strengths for the benefit of the business. We are looking for people who can contribute in ways that make us better at what we do, for that is always the ultimate competitive advantage. What can that potential new hire bring to this company? I have a question that I ask of every person I interview. Typically, it stops people cold in their tracks: "I want you to tell me three things of true, measurable business value that you will bring to our business that will convince me that I should hire you over the other candidates. Your answers can't be 'I'm honest, I show up on time, or I'm hardworking'; I don't need to hear any of those. They are just generalities and platitudes, like mom, baseball, hot dogs, and apple pie. If you come to work here, what are you going to deliver (not do) that improves our business's performance, health, and culture?"

What I am looking for is someone who says, "Here are three things that I will bring into this business that you're either not doing today and you want to do or that you're not doing well, and I can help improve your performance." That shows me someone who has done their homework about the business I lead and who is prepared to make a contribution.

Then, of course, I expect them to deliver. That's their commitment. We carefully word our offer letters so that they don't simply express what we want a new team member to do; we describe in measurable terms what we expect them to *achieve*. A new employee's signature on the offer letter is not simply an official indication that they have accepted the job; they are signing their name indicating their commitment to get the job done. There's a difference. Commitment is why I stopped using the title of department head and changed it to business owner, for I want individuals who have an owner's mentality and treat the portion of the business that falls under their purview with such an approach. I expect them to mentally and physically own their area of responsibility within the business and to be accountable for attaining or exceeding the performance targets assigned to their specific role, department, or business unit. This is nothing more than the embodiment of the balance of empowerment and accountability. I remind them that if they accept the offer of employment, rather than them adopting the perspective that they are coming to work for me, I actually now work for them, because they have signed up to take ownership and responsibility for the area of the business for which they are being hired. They are to lead the charge in that discipline or department, not me. I work for them in the context that they can ask me to participate and help them when there is an obstacle in their path keeping them from achieving the defined objectives, and in that particular instance, the best person to mitigate or remove that obstacle is me. I explain to them that no job is what it appears like from the outside looking in, and they will probably experience a "Sixth Monday Crisis of Belief." This is a phenomenon that occurs about five weeks after somebody starts a new job, and at the beginning of the sixth week, they are standing in front of their bathroom mirror shaving or fixing their hair, and they say to themselves, "What was I thinking? Why did I take this job?" This happens with almost every new role any of us ever takes. It's new, it's scary, and it's not what we thought it was. No job is. But I tell a new employee that they have to push through the "Sixth Monday Crisis of Belief" and not let it deter them. I tell them that I expect them to be at our company for a minimum of one year, because it takes that long for the individual to settle in and for the role to settle out; only then do both parties—the employer and the employee—know if this is a long-term fit. I tell them that if they can't commit to own the performance targets and to stay here through the good and the bad for a full year, then they should not sign the offer, and we can part friends and go get some lunch. No hard feelings. Better to part ways now than later after it has cost both parties time, effort, and money.

If they do sign their letters, then the next-to-last (chemistry is last) of the seven Cs I expect from them, and something I have diligently tried to assess in advance, is their sincere interest in being a collaborative teammate. I have spoken at length elsewhere about the importance of collaboration, so I won't belabor the point here other than to say that I view this ability as so essential to our business's success that it is central to our hiring process.

Of course, if team members are going to be successful collaborators, they need to be skilled communicators, something that is becoming ever more challenging and that is the subject I will address next.

MANTRAS FOR EXCELLENCE:

O Digital communication is ideal for conveying information, but it is not very effective when resolving
differences.

O "Clarity trumps persuasion." —Tim Pecoraro

O In business, in the long run, verbal communication is
the same as no communication at all. Write it down!

Chapter 19

DIGITAL COMMUNICATION
AND THE DEMISE OF
GENUINE DIALOGUE

Perhaps you are like me. I continue to think that the ever-growing misuse of digital communication will decline and that one day we will realize the inefficiencies, miscommunication, and relational damage that can result from the inappropriate and ill-timed use of all forms of digital communication: email, texting, Slack, social media—the list continues to grow. The reality is that overuse has in many instances turned into misuse and abuse. It's one of those ironies you realize when you step back and examine the big shifts that take place in culture—business culture and social culture—that the technological tools that were supposed to make us more efficient and bring us closer together sometimes do the opposite. We desperately need to regain our appreciation for in-person, face-to-face—and even phone—interactions and discourse. Every day I see the erosion of our ability as a society to negotiate an acceptable common position when two parties are not in alignment with each other, many times because we are not willing or are afraid to engage in meaningful, real-time dialogue with the people with whom we may be at odds in reaching an equitable solution.

Frequently, I encourage a colleague to contact another party to collect a late receivable, secure a resource in a timely fashion, or settle a disagreement or dispute only to inquire a week later and hear, "Well, I sent them an email, but I haven't heard from them yet." Basically, an entire week has passed with no substantive ground gained against an issue that could have been resolved in an hour or less. I believe we are dealing with a cultural reality that we have not faced before, in that many of us spend as much time, if not far more, interacting with digital devices as we do with humans. What I have long seen as problematic has become a kind of epidemic with the significant shift to virtual or remote work environments, especially with the appearance and long-term implications and impact of COVID-19. And once you let the horse out of the barn, the vestiges of that tectonic shift certainly look like they will be firmly etched into the architecture and operation of our commercial ecosystems for the foreseeable future and maybe longer.

> **We are dealing with a cultural reality that we have not faced before, in that many of us spend as much time, if not far more, interacting with digital devices as we do with humans.**

Generally, digital devices behave in a logical fashion. When I press the *s* key on the keyboard, an *s* appears on the screen. When I pull my smartphone out of my pocket, I expect it to perform flawlessly and in the same manner every time. In fact, on the rare occasion when our digital devices don't work or are out of service or range, we usually are completely flabbergasted and sometimes furious. One hundred percent availability and predictability are the standards in today's digital world.

The problem is that those same characteristics and parameters are not always congruent with human nature and the human experience. The digital-centric communication culture of today begs the need to make a clear distinction between the digital world and the world of flesh and bone, tissue and sinew, heart and soul and mind. The digital world is logical and linear. Humans, however, not so much. Humans are, in fact, somewhat random. Humans are individuals. Unlike the latest version of the iPhone—a single model with millions of exact duplicates—no two of us are exactly alike. We emanate from a wide range of cultures, upbringings, and circumstances, and we espouse different perspectives, wants, and needs. We do not all act or react in the same way, and we are not always predictable. We do not all arrive at the same conclusions at the same time, and in many cases, we will not arrive at the same conclusion at any time. Ever.

Digital communication is appropriate when we are communicating things we know, and in some cases, things we need, but it is usually not fitting for issues being negotiated. Digital communication is ideal for conveying information, but it is not very effective when resolving differences. Digital communication may inaccurately convey tone and emotion and in many cases is misused when the author projects a counterfeit air of authority or power because they can do so when operating behind the faceless veil of digital copy and transmission. However, when these same individuals are forced to engage in face-to-face discussion, they quickly retreat to a much softer position with a compromised proclamation, delivered with no real conviction, exposing them for the power pretenders that, in many cases, they really are.

In addition, digital media is challenged to serve as an effective platform for rich dialogue. In fact, I would categorize digital communication as a serial monologue of sorts. First, you say or post something, then I respond, then you respond, then I say or post something, and it goes on from there. Real conversations and discussions inherently include interruptions, uncomfortable pauses, emotions, exclamations, and redirects interspersed throughout the process, making the dialogue sometimes none too efficient but rich and real and effective. Our digital devices and digital media in many cases have eroded from assets to liabilities. How often have you had to call a team meeting simply to clear up a mess that started with a digital misunderstanding? How many hours have you lost to trying to placate the feelings of a team member who expresses frustration with a colleague, only to find that the root of the problem resides in a misunderstood email, text, or internal chat? I submit that if we accurately accounted the time spent composing, posting, responding, clarifying, responding again, and confirming, in many cases we would find that not only was digital communication not effective at achieving the desired result or effect but also that it was inefficient, taking more time and effort than traditional in-person or phone communication.

It has been said that the measure of a truly successful negotiation is that neither party gets exactly what they want but that the parties find a common ground that each can accept. As my friend Tim Pecoraro—a leader, a communicator, and an artist—always reminds me, "clarity trumps persuasion" every time. Today, it seems to me the more sensitive the subject matter or tougher the negotiation or greater the philosophical distance between two parties, the more we resort to some form of digital transmission that is marginally effective at bringing two parties in accord with one another. Effective interpersonal communication requires skill, with an element of art mixed in.

Our choice of appropriate communication mediums is not an either/or dilemma; it is a both/and decision. We live in a diverse, technology-centric culture that demands the mastery of many skills in order to fulfill our potential and achieve significance. We can't effectively communicate everything that needs communicating via emojis. In yet another irony, despite the presence of a myriad of digital mediums, channels, and platforms, and the integration of video, audio, memes, emojis, and other features, the vast majority of digital communication is still text. Entered one letter at a time. How inefficient is that? We had better learn how to write well and in a clear and concise manner. And we better be in the habit of communicating the results (output and outcomes) of those face-to-face negotiations and decisions in writing, or else we fail the analog reality that in business, verbal communication is the same as no communication at all. Two weeks from now, you're going to say I said it one way and I am going to say I said it another. Four weeks from now, you're going to say I said it, and I am going to say that I didn't say it at all. Write it down! Our reality is that we may live in a digital world, but we interact and work with humans. No matter how much we may depend on digital technology now or in the future, our businesses will still be driven by our people, and that means we have to master the both/and of communicating humanly and digitally. Learn to match the communication medium with each type of situation you encounter to maximize clarity, knowledge transfer, and productivity while minimizing ambiguity, inefficiency, and hurt feelings.

I will continue to fully exploit my digital devices, but I am not going to discard your phone number or physical address. I

Our reality is that we may live in a digital world, but we interact and work with humans.

need those, just as I need the camaraderie, stories, lessons, advice, and laughter that inevitably accompany the half dozen or more meals I share a week with colleagues, customers, associates, and friends.

MANTRAS FOR EXCELLENCE:

○ Technically priceless but practically worthless.

○ There is no price, even free, that makes something that is a poor fit or of marginal quality a good value.

○ Almost every choice we make in life either expands or contracts our realm of possibilities.

○ Execute as quickly as you can without compromising the quality of the outcome or the output.

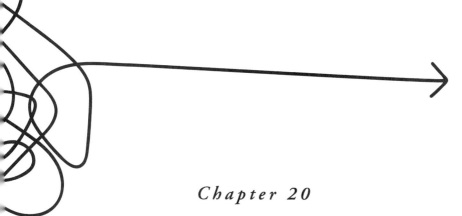

TECHNICALLY PRICELESS BUT
PRACTICALLY WORTHLESS

It has been a long time ago now, but I remember when my dad was about to retire from Guilford Mills where he was vice president of engineering, and he began hiring additional engineers to replace him and to augment the staff that he would leave behind. He came home for more than a few days in a row in less than the best of moods after the retooled engineering team had been in place for a few months. I asked him what was going on, and he explained that a few of the newer, less experienced engineers were really bright and were up to speed on the latest computer-based graphic design and engineering analysis tools. "So," I asked, "what's the problem then?" He explained that his department had made a sizable investment in new technology and software when the new engineers first arrived on the scene, and now that the company was in its annual budget cycle preparing for the next fiscal year, the same engineers had requested another sizable capital investment in additional software. The problem, he said, was that they had not utilized or leveraged much of the capabilities in the software that had been licensed and installed the year before. The company had yet to experience any significant operational or financial benefits as a result of the initial investment. Pop told these young engineers that he was not making any more investment in systems or software until they more fully utilized the capabilities already at their disposal and their use of the tools began to positively impact the productivity and profitability of the company. This is Pop's line that I will never forget when he described the underutilized software investment: "technically priceless but practically worthless."

We're probably all guilty of spending money on programs and products that are not making money for our companies. Yes, we have very good theoretical and technical reasons and arguments as to why we are doing what we are doing, but the results are simply not there. Remember, the numbers don't lie.

Imagine if Pop ran a tire shop instead of overseeing an engineering division and he had bought every technician in the shop a pneumatic torque wrench. Would he believe his shop or his customers were in good hands if he found his crews all employing hand tools? Because his engineers weren't using anywhere near the full capabilities of the technology they had been provided, he had every reason to wonder where else they might be falling short. Did they treat application of their skill and knowledge with the same partial embrace they demonstrated toward the technology provided to make them more productive and efficient? Were they of the mind that simply spending money provided the means to attain objectives? There is no price, even free, that makes something that is a poor fit or of marginal quality a good value.

Let's say that whether it's tires or engineering services or one of a thousand other business opportunities, you have done your due diligence and you are confident that there is justification for introducing a new product or service to increase sales and market penetration. You know what you're doing, as the success of your business can attest. The data supports your conclusions. You've got your ducks in a row. Yet let's say that this time you fail, and the initiative doesn't produce results. There can be only three possible reasons for that failure. One, you are offering the wrong product or service. That thing you were convinced customers wanted…well, you missed the mark. They want something else. Two, if your assessment of the situation leaves you convinced that you've got the right product or service customers want and your view is corroborated by outside market research and intelligence, then you've got the wrong process. You have entered or approached the market in the wrong way. Or you have deployed the wrong promotional plan. Perhaps you've chosen the wrong distribution partners or taken the wrong sales approach. If your assessment further reveals that the process is not the culprit, that leaves the third reason standing alone. Assuming that you have evidence to suggest that customers want your product and that your approach to the market is sound, then what's left? Only one thing. You've got the wrong people doing it.

It used to be that the common business model for optimization was PPT—people, process, technology—in that order. Then, with the onset of the Toyota Production System, Six Sigma, lean, and continuous improvement initiatives, the optimization model changed order and shifted to process, people, technology, where the number one thing was to optimize the process and then find the personnel who could execute and improve the process from that point forward. After those two variables were addressed, then we could identify and deploy the technology that would allow us to enforce and execute the processes as designed. Today, however, I would submit that the order of PPT has necessarily changed again. Now it is PTP: process, technology, people, with process and technology running together virtually concurrently. If I throw people or technology at a bad process, we're just going to make mistakes faster. The reality is that technology is at the core of almost every business process that we execute. And today's advanced technologies don't just automate or enforce processes that we have already designed; they actually enable new processes that simply could not be performed without the technology. So finding and operating the right technology is an important component of all continuous improvement programs. We need software, process automation, artificial intelligence, and robotics that are a good fit for our current operating model but that are flexible enough to support the adjustments needed as we improve our

> The reality is that technology is at the core of almost every business process that we execute.

processes to meet the demands of tomorrow. Because of the rapidly changing commercial, social, and digital world in which we exist, I have replaced the notion of best practices with the term *prevailing* practices. The best practice today is old news tomorrow, so we have to stay on our toes and realize that nothing stays in the "best" category very long. Being mentally and physically agile enables us to adjust when a prevailing practice is no longer optimum for what we are trying to achieve.

All applications must be practical and effective. In other words, they have to help us achieve the goals and directives of the organization. They cannot simply be rules that we blindly follow. The technologies we apply, including information technology, must be measured by their ability to improve operational and financial performance, and that means our people must not only be able to apply them but also to extract the full potential out of the tool or technology being employed. If that's not the case, then we may be falling in love with shiny objects that we can't put to work. Sometimes you make money by not making that investment you think you need to make. The reality is that many things on which we spend money in our businesses don't help us make more money.

We have to make the hard decisions to stop spending/investing where it doesn't matter and redirect our resources toward the business opportunities that hold the greatest potential to generate profits and increase business value. When analyzing things like expenditure or investment decisions, it is worth remembering that almost every choice we make in life either expands or contracts our realm of possibilities. In our business, we judiciously review every purchase or capital expenditure request of any magnitude to see if it is worth its weight in salt. We have documented and utilize a fairly lengthy set of qualification criteria to determine whether a purchase request is worthy of our investment. The six summary-level questions that we ask ourselves follow:

- Will it generate profitable revenue?

- Will it reduce or delay cost?

- Will it increase productivity?

- Will it reduce or eliminate waste or rework (i.e., improve quality)?

- Will it shorten material/product lead time?

- Will it improve customer satisfaction and/or retention?

This is the first line of scrutiny that every investment/spend proposal must pass. An opportunity does not need to achieve all six criteria to be approved as a candidate for investment, but it must achieve at least one, and most times more than one, to move to the next round of consideration.

Asking these questions provides a simple process that gives us a *first cut* at eliminating waste from our business and directing our resources toward activities and programs that matter. From there we can move on to assessing investments at the next level, applying what I like to call business process and systems bull factors.

THE "BULL" FACTORS

Will the process or system change we are contemplating meet the test of being

- availa*bull*?
- scala*bull*?
- flexi*bull*?
- managea*bull*?
- relia*bull*?
- applica*bull*?
- maintana*bull*?
- integrata*bull*?
- upgrada*bull*?
- repeata*bull*?
- dependa*bull*?
- adapta*bull*?
- profita*bull*?

In the competitive environments we face today, the method for optimizing most processes (and most products for that matter) comes through applied technologies in the form of innovation. Most innovation comes in the form of combining common things in unique ways.

Innovations have to meet most or all these bull factors because their job is to optimize processes and products.

A primary goal of innovative technology is to enable us to execute a process as quickly as we can without compromising the quality of the outcome or the output. Innovation practicality means the innovation has to work and it has to be understandable, because in order to produce the desired output, it can't be so complicated that it becomes an administrative nightmare to manage, execute, or measure. In this way, we come full circle, for if an innovation cannot be practical, then it cannot help expediate processes that pass the bull test, and we're right back to where we started: technically priceless but practically worthless.

In the competitive environments we face today, the method for optimizing most processes (and most products for that matter) comes through applied technologies in the form of innovation.

PART 4

SALES EXCELLENCE: CUSTOMERS DON'T WANT TO BE SOLD; THEY WANT TO BE SERVED

MANTRAS FOR EXCELLENCE:

- People love to buy but hate to be sold.

- No one ever regretted buying the best.

- People buy from you because they believe you understand their business.

- Just say no.

- Customers want guidance, not options.

- Customers don't want to be sold; they want to be served.

Chapter 21

THE REVERSE-NEGATIVE
SELLING MODEL

We can achieve organizational excellence among our teams, within our culture, and in how we communicate internally, and none of it matters if we don't transact business in a way that enables the organization to be profitable and grow. And one fact of business is that not much happens in business until something gets sold. In my experience, all good sales approaches contemplate the fact that people love to buy but hate to be sold. That reality has led me to what I label the reverse negative selling model. The very title suggests something important, for I believe that people and companies that make quantum leaps often apply counterintuitive or reverse thinking to their most fundamental business operations. Often it's time well spent to identify a problem and then approach it from the exact opposite way convention tells us we should. Let me give you an example of what I mean.

Early on in my career when I was a regional salesperson for IBM, there were core principles officially installed and enforced by IBM that I took fully to heart (still do, as a matter of fact). One was this: Never disparage your competition. After I left IBM, I joined the leadership team of a small but growing software firm, Jobscope, that developed software for capital equipment manufacturers. Not too many months into my tenure there, I had a sales prospect who was trying to decide between Jobscope and one of our competitors. The prospect raised concerns about our company and our software product that he had heard from the other primary competitor vying for his business. He shared with me a number of negative "facts" of which he had been made aware that gave him pause about proceeding with us. After he finished sharing his perspectives, he said to me, "They told me a bunch of stuff about you. What can you tell me about them?"

> People and companies that make quantum leaps often apply counterintuitive or reverse thinking to their most fundamental business operations.

I replied, "To be honest, I don't know an awful lot about the inner workings of their company or their product. There are only so many hours in a day, and rather than spend my time focusing on everything my competition is doing right or wrong, my time is better spent understanding how your business works, what type of automation and technology you need to operate and scale your business, and making sure that I propose the modules and features of our software that hold the greatest potential to help you streamline your manufacturing process to increase productivity and profitability. I just can't speak to the competition. And if I could, I wouldn't say anything negative about them." I seemed to stun him into silence, and we ended our phone call with him telling me that he was going to do a little more research and would call me back in a few days with his decision.

About a week later, he called me back. "Well, I made my decision." When I inquired what it was, he said, "I didn't have to make a decision. I really didn't have a choice. It's simple. All your competitor talked about was your company and your software. And all you talked about was your company and your software. So I really only know about your company and your software, so I'm buying from you!"

I share that story because it speaks to at least two different principles at once: (1) going against what is expected or viewed as convention can pay dividends, and (2) always stay true to your values. The application of these two principles may feel backward, as was the case in this story, about how many salespeople approach the sales process. Going against convention isn't really about *being* different, but it is about *thinking* in different patterns. It's not about doing something different; it's about doing something better. For example, one of my core beliefs about sales is extraordinarily simple: No one ever regretted buying the best. Think about it. Remember the first time you bought a new car with heated seats only because it was part of the equipment package on the vehicle you wanted that was on the lot? Now tell me the next time you were in the market for a new car, you didn't make sure it had heated seats? You might not love paying more for them, but you weren't going to do without them once you experienced them, right? I have challenged every business I've ever led to identify the things that only it can do and then do those things better than anyone else. If I can be confident that's the case, selling gets a lot easier.

That concept takes me to the heart of the first part of reverse negative selling, the *reverse* part. Believe it or not, the sales processes I have promoted for many years actually require the prospect to do more work than the salesperson. When I was with OOBE, every two weeks like clockwork, we sent, or in some cases delivered in person, a questionnaire to a very large uniform prospect. It was a sizable questionnaire, one that contained some of the most in-depth, erudite questions you can imagine, right down to the type of cloth they preferred, styling questions, closure mechanisms, accessories. You name it. We sent these questionnaires on the principle that when prospects invest time, energy, and money with a potential supplier, they begin to value that potential supplier relationship because they have invested so much in it, even before the relationship is formalized. By spending substantial time addressing our questions, two things occurred: They spent that time focused on *us*, and it kept them from thinking about or interacting with our competition. From our end, the time they spent allowed us to gauge how much our company and our proposal actually mattered to them. Rather than me trying to tell a customer what it is I can provide them, reverse selling makes them tell me what it is they think they need. By asking insightful questions, I can extract from them exactly what they are trying to achieve. I learn their business. Sometimes it's just a matter of playing their own words back to them, things like "Here's what you told us were your biggest challenges. This is what you told me about how your process works." People buy from you because they believe you understand their business.

I've made a living selling by not selling. I don't wish to be misunderstood, but I really do believe that just as we have to earn our customers' sales, our customers have to "qualify" to do business with us by sharing exactly what it is they are trying to accomplish and demonstrating that they have identified what is truly important to their business. I want to know that they have analyzed what is working in their business and what is not, that they have spent energy on identifying what it is they want to achieve and how the products and services (i.e., solutions) we have at our disposal might help them accomplish it. If I don't make the customer answer those questions, I will have nothing to go on other than surface-level information. That type of information is a lot like topsoil—it covers the earth, but it's not very deep. That level of information rarely has the depth to provide any real insight into what will truly transform their business. If they don't have a grasp on what is most important to them, I can't sell them something that will help them get there. At the end of the day, I haven't spent my career selling software, or hardware, or uniforms, or manufacturing equipment; ultimately what I've sold is business performance improvement.

And here's the *negative* part of reverse negative selling; embrace what Nancy Reagan advised us to do in a major public affairs campaign to end teen drug use during her husband's administration: "Just say no." Salespeople the world over are famous for promising the moon. "Can your product defy the laws of nature and look good doing it?" "Why, yes, ma'am, it certainly does." When salespeople are placed in pressure situations, "Yes" becomes their default answer because they think it's what the customer wants to hear and because they are fearful that their competitor can deliver something they can't. It's sad to say, but many salespeople know only five words: "Yes, we can do that."

I've bucked this tradition and trained my salespeople to just say no to every fifth question. "Can you sell me your product for ten percent less than what you told me is your best price?" "I'm sorry, I can't do that." I don't care if the fifth question asked of my salesperson is, "Do you need to use the restroom?" I want their answer to be no. Okay, that instruction is given a little bit tongue in cheek to create impact, but you get the point. I'd rather they reply, "I know our competition says they can do that, but we don't. I understand what you are trying to achieve, and the solution or service the competition is proposing is what most of our competitors do, but we offer a different approach." So it's not just no; it's no, but… In addition, we need to say no to things we don't do, because if we don't, the customer is ultimately going to be disappointed. If I'm straight with them, not only do they know where they stand and where we stand, but over time, if I am able to make an improvement in a product, shorten lead time, extend our customer service hours, and provide them more than I promised, they will recognize our integrity and know that they can trust us.

Here's an easy example of what I mean. I had a prospect who asked us to commit that we would ship orders on the day they were received so long as their orders were posted by 3:00 p.m. I told them we couldn't do that. I explained that to be entirely certain we maintained accuracy and quality while working within the limitations of our shipping partners, we could only promise same-day delivery for orders placed by noon. It was entirely likely that we had competitors making a 3:00 p.m. promise, but I was sincere in my reasons for why that was not always possible. I told the customer, "We can't meet your three p.m. request today, but we will work with our logistics partners and adjust processes as we can to see if we can't gradually extend the order placement deadline for same-day shipment. I can't make you a promise that I can't keep." At the end of the day, our customer appreciated our honesty. What happened? We won the business. And within eighteen months, we were able to ship orders that were received by 3:00 p.m. the same day.

The business model that I have espoused, deployed, and operated has always been pretty simple when it comes right down to it: Strive for excellence. If a customer chooses to do business with us, they expect us to be transparent about how we work and what we can and cannot do. They've trusted that we know our own ballpark. And we do. We know where all the sprinkler heads are so that we don't trip up unexpectedly. We can put an X on every gopher hole in the outfield. We know exactly where the right field foul line deviates two inches toward the bleachers so that we know where and how to get a hit when our competition hits a foul ball. When you start trying to shape your company against the competition's blueprint instead of what the customer needs and within the limits of what you have the actual capacity to do, you're playing in somebody else's ballpark. Don't be afraid to think counterintuitively, to figure out what your unique value proposition is, and then always express it in terms that matter to your customer.

Most vendors and suppliers operate in a subservient position to the customer. The default position is "Thank you for seeing me today." Customers want a worthy partner. But they also want a worthy adversary. If you don't ever challenge their thinking, you're not bringing them anything. In order to create relationships where you challenge your customers sufficiently so that they believe that you understand their business and bring them value, you've got to be able to back it up. Reverse negative selling can't and won't work if you have no substance. You've got to be able to bring the E^2: experience and expertise. Customers want guidance, not options. Don't lay out an Easter basket full of colored egg choices and let the customer simply pick out the ones they like; that is order-taking, not selling. Customers want to know that we have acted as their agent—that we have vetted all the high-potential solutions and distilled those down to the one or two that truly hold the most value for them. Understand enough about what your prospects and customers are trying to achieve

> Don't be afraid to think counterintuitively, to figure out what your unique value proposition is, and then always express it in terms that matter to your customer.

so that you can provide guidance that directs them to the choice(s) that will deliver the greatest benefits. Once your customer accepts you as the expert, a trusted advisor, an authority, they'll call you for *every-thing* because they know that if you can't do it, you'll connect them to somebody who can. In my version of sales excellence, if I can't provide my customer something that can bring them a competitive advantage, then we'll shake hands, share a lunch, and I'll send them to someone who can. My job is to help my customer operate their business more productively and more profitably. Customers don't want to be sold; they want to be served.

The reverse-negative sales model leverages two important aspects of a true customer *service* model, one built upon experience, instincts, and values. It's an excellent starting point, but to *excel* at sales, you have to understand the science behind selling, which is where we will go next.

MANTRAS FOR EXCELLENCE:

O   The greatest tool salespeople have at their disposal is their brain.

O   Consistent sales success requires nearly flawless planning and execution. One without the other is useless.

O   Never negotiate at the negotiating table.

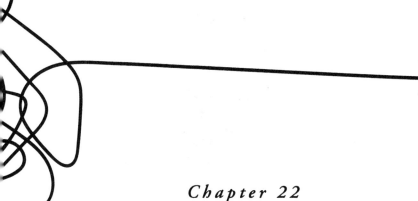

Chapter 22

SALES IS A SCIENCE, NOT A SCIENCE PROJECT

Effective salespeople make sales. Now most of us carry some scars from dealing with insufferable salespeople—the classic metaphor of the used car salesman comes to mind—an experience with someone who will do anything, say anything, and promise anything to close a sale. Many of us have also developed a lack of trust and a degree of skepticism when we deal with truly engaging salespeople—those about whom it has been said, "They could sell ice to Eskimos." Maybe they are too charismatic, too charming, and their clothes, hair, and watches are just too perfect. Both extremes prompt us to elevate our defenses—raise our guards—but the reality is that neither perception is accurate. Neither representation contemplates the reality that making sales is a science, not a science project.

Effective selling begins with finding high-quality prospects. You can get everything else right in the balance of the selling equation—great sales talent quarterbacking the sale, a perfectly planned and executed sales process, and even a prospect who operates within an industry that you know and serve well—but if the prospect does not have a pressing need that is critical to its success, a reasonable budgetary amount assigned to addressing that need, a sense of urgency to address the need now, and concurrence among the entire buying group that the solution you are offering is a priority, the chances of you making a near-term sale are virtually nil. If you do make the

Effective selling begins with finding high-quality prospects.

sale, it is probably because someone with buying/budget authority made a snap decision because they like you or didn't have the fortitude to tell you no and stop the process, at least for the time being. The best salespeople understand that you can't transform a grade C lead into a grade A prospect. The temptation of most garden-variety salespeople when they have an anemic sales pipeline is to go back through their old prospects and try to reinitiate a dialogue with an account with whom they have had previous contact that didn't materialize into a sale. Sometimes this approach works, but most times the payback is not worth the effort. My experience has taught me that *before* my sales pipeline begins to look like a desert, the best way I can spend my time is to diligently and rigorously prospect with the objective of identifying new grade A prospects. This is not an easy or fun exercise many times, and it takes discipline. I call this the hard slogging of prospecting, but more than any other activity or element of a successful sales process, successful prospecting is the key to sales success.

Second, the best salespeople are what I call P^2 Zen masters. P^2 stands for predictability and punctuality. The best salespeople know which sales they are going to make, and they know when they are going to close them. This is true because they prospect continuously, rigorously qualify each lead they uncover, and devote the majority of their time and effort to prospects and sales opportunities that meet their ideal customer criteria and that they can win. They waste little time or attention on marginally qualified leads. I have said for years that I want to win only my fair share of sales opportunities—and that is *all* of them! That sounds arrogant, but it is not. I try to rigorously disqualify all marginal sales opportunities so that my sales pipeline includes only sales that we ought to win and that we can win. When you qualify first and qualify hard, only then do you apply sales effort and a winning sales process to those accounts that make it through your qualification filter. If you do that, your win rate will go through the roof.

What first-level filter do you use to qualify a prospect? I start with an acronym: NTSB (and no, I'm not talking about the National Transportation Safety Board). NTSB in sales translates to Need + Timing + Sponsorship + Budget. All legitimate near-term sales opportunities inherently exhibit all four criteria. Is there a legitimate need for the product or service because it addresses a pressing challenge or enables the business to capitalize on a lucrative market opportunity? Is the timing right? Is the consumer or the business committed to securing a solution *now* because every day that passes costs money or market share? Is there sponsorship and support across all influencers and decision makers? Will the budget of the target prospect's organization support an expenditure of the necessary magnitude? If *one* of these essential elements is missing, the account may represent a longer-term business development opportunity, but your chances of closing a near-term sale are slim.

The materialization of most new sales opportunities begins with one or more of the three Rs: reputation, referrals, and relationships. Let's start with the last *R*: relationships. Remember the mantra I shared earlier? All long-term relationships, business or personal, require two fundamental ingredients: trust and respect. What your prospect is really looking for is not personality; they want prescriptive guidance— a carefully architected set of recommendations fueled by an insightful understanding of their business. Historically, sales has been considered a visceral activity fueled by passion, a competitive spirit, a fast internal motor, an elevated level of intuition (i.e., long antennas), and a need to win, but it was not a role that demanded an uncommon level of intelligence and an analytical mind. The fact is that the greatest tool salespeople have at their disposal is their brain. Sometimes we forget that. Sales is an inherently competitive portion of the business, and it can be easy to get caught up in the atmosphere of competition and forget that outthinking your competitors is your surest path to success. One of the primary differences between intelligent individuals and less intelligent individuals is that intelligent people have a penchant for and an ability to solve problems. Especially complex problems with multiple variables. When many salespeople encounter obstacles in the sales process that they have not faced before, it paralyzes them, and they either give up or resort to proposing canned solutions that have worked in similar situations. The intelligent salesperson recognizes the breadth and depth of resources at their disposal, and their response is, "*We* will figure this out." If you can't look to your own experience for previous sales success in similar situations or find readily available solutions by utilizing the resources within your line of sight, look more broadly. The legacy view that the resources, employees, and solutions that exist within the four walls of our facilities represent the totality of our capabilities and capacity is defunct. When we encounter a sales opportunity that we can win, but we don't have all of the capabilities or capacity that we need to win, then we draw upon a well-architected and established network of alliances and partnerships, and we *assemble* the ideal solution for our client. We are the system or solutions integrator, the conduit through which the total, seamless solution gets proposed, sold, and delivered. Today, no organization can be an expert in every discipline inherent in the industry verticals that they serve—information technology, retail, life sciences, marketing, consumer products, you name it. The areas of business, and life, in which we can truly be an expert get narrower every day. The key to winning large sales opportunities, becoming more vertically integrated, and achieving market leader status is many times the breadth and strength of your alliances and partnerships.

Good salespeople are hard to find and even harder to hire. I have heard the term *four percenter* used to describe the best salespeople. That term derives from a perspective that 90 percent of the stuff sold in the world is sold by 4 percent of the world's salespeople. Those are the ones you want to find, hire, and keep. How do you find them? Ask your customers and suppliers for the names of the best salespeople who call on them. Ask for their contact information, or better yet, request a warm introduction. As Peter Drucker said, "In the absence of other evidence, the best indicator of future performance is past performance." Find a sales leader with a proven track record. The industry in which they were successfully selling may matter, but many times it does not. It *does* make a difference if the salesperson you are considering has spent their career selling products versus selling services. Those two sales approaches can be very different. Somebody who has been selling products is selling something with definable dimensions and

> The key to winning large sales opportunities, becoming more vertically integrated, and achieving market leader status is many times the breadth and strength of your alliances and partnerships.

characteristics (reads, feeds, and speeds). Somebody who sells services is selling an idea—a better way of life for the client. A variety of services may have to be customized, tailored, amalgamated, and integrated to craft the final end solution that the client ultimately purchases. Many times, product salespeople do not make good services salespeople and vice versa, so take this into consideration when recruiting the sales leadership and the sales force that you need.

Remember the old saying that he who aims at nothing always hits it? You've got to be able to think like your customer, which means you've got to do your homework. Information is readily available, so dig in, pull from multiple sources, find out everything you can. When outstanding questions still remain, ask your prospect. More important than having all the right answers is asking intelligent, insightful questions. Your prospect will appreciate your desire to understand their world. Too many salespeople fail to recognize that the *real* work starts before ever meeting with the customer. You're not selling a product or a service; you are selling business performance improvement. To understand how our solutions can materially improve the performance and health of a client's operation, we must first understand the prospect's operation at a detailed level. Only then can we paint an accurate picture of how our solutions connect with our prospect's business in a way that improves operational and financial performance.

The simple reality is that what most customers are looking for is pretty straightforward. The approach Staples took when they used the idea of the "EASY" button in a sales campaign suggests some simple, central elements of a sales model:

- The seller needs for the product or service *to be easy to* explain, sell, install, and support.

- The customer wants the product or service *to be easy to* understand, buy, use, and maintain.

When you stop worrying about being likable and instead figure out how to address the customer's needs, you will realize there is almost always a way to make the sale. Neither you nor your customer enter the relationship looking for a friend. They need a solution. You want a sale. When you get on their page and begin to work together, real friendships many times develop. But it doesn't begin there. As Adam Landrum, founder and CEO of the Up & Up Agency in Greenville shared with me a few years back, the supplier/customer relationship usually proceeds along the following progression: Stranger » Acquaintance » Customer » Advocate (SACA).

If the prospect passes the NTSB test, there is another acronym that provides some criteria that need to be met to consistently secure the sale opportunities that you are pursuing. I didn't come up with this model and the associated acronym, as somebody shared this with me years ago, but it resonated with me, and it has always stuck. The acronym is MEDDIC. Think *medic* spelled wrong. MEDDIC represents a few critical elements of a sales process that are mandatory and that cannot be trivialized or bypassed if you want to close sales in a predictable and punctual (P^2) manner. Not knowing and including all of the following in your sales process/cycle probably means you were simply lucky if you happen to win:

- *Metric*: Know the value proposition you are proposing to meet their needs. Be prepared to demonstrate, concretely, why your approach can provide them a return on investment. Have on hand a comparable success story that will resonate with your customer.

- *Economic* buyer: You need to meet and get to know the person (CEO, CFO, COO, etc.) who has to give a thumbs-up to the business case. Is the cost-benefit ratio favorable enough to warrant the expenditure? Who has the authority to say no and is the key individual you have to get to say yes?

- *Decision* process: What process does the sale need to follow? What committees or buying groups need to sign off to make it happen?

- *Decision* criteria: How will the prospect declare a winner? Are they measuring all contenders via a requirements scorecard, an evaluation, a product demonstration, a proof-of-concept exercise, a pilot, etc.?

- *Identify* pain: You need to be aware of a prevailing pain that makes your prospect want or need to act. What problem are they looking to solve? What loss are they needing to cover? What process do they have that is broken?

- *Champion*: You need to develop or identify a champion within the prospect organization, the person who, at some point in the sales process, will put their neck on the line for you. We're not talking about a sponsor or a coach within the organization who is your primary contact or the one who is supposed to shepherd the sale through their process but the person who will step up and help advocate for why you are their greatest hope.

Adhere faithfully to these sales principles and approaches, and you don't need luck. In fact, the responsible, strategic salesperson rigorously *disqualifies* all leads and prospects for which the chances of winning are low. This is why the best salespeople don't just win their fair share of deals; they win all of them. That's somewhat of an exaggeration—but not by much. They win because they have done their homework, know their prospect, have worked diligently to establish a relationship built on trust and respect, and manage the sales process so that it does not elongate and the sale is closed in a timely manner. Time kills all deals. The longer a sale goes unclosed, the greater the opportunity for bad things to occur that can derail or kill the sale. In short, consistent sales success requires virtually flawless planning *and* execution. One without the other is useless.

Still sound impossible, to win all the deals? Well, world-class salespeople possess a number of other qualities and stick to a few key principles, viewing them as essential elements of a detailed strategic process. They are highly persuasive but never pushy. That lack of pushiness originates with honest respect for the customer. They know you can't make a sale until somebody is ready to buy. They base their answers to customer questions on facts and data. They are articulate and accurate, understanding that clarity trumps cool every day of the week. While they don't rely on charisma, they are socially adept and learn how to read their customers. And they know how to close a deal. When the customer wants to negotiate, they don't agree to alternative terms that they have not fully contemplated in advance. Never negotiate at the negotiating table. Only present or accept terms that have been previously considered and internally validated and accepted prior to the negotiation discussion. They also follow an old sales maxim when concessions are being requested: never give something away without getting something in return.

In those rare instances when their carefully architected sales plan doesn't work, many times because of circumstances that are unforeseeable or beyond their control, world-class salespeople know not to burn bridges when a sale is lost. The best prospects many times are second-time-around prospects. When a former prospect revisits your offerings after a disappointing experience with your competitor, you stand a good chance of winning their business in a fairly short period of time because they already know you, and the sales cycle can many times be abbreviated.

The most important element of your value proposition is your *only* statement. Think in terms of the following: "We are the *only* company that _____." What can you offer that no one else can provide, or even better, that no one else can even claim? Describe and demonstrate for your prospect how your *only* statement is essential to their success. Define the measurable operational and financial improvements your solution will provide your potential customer. This ability to define your *only* statement is what I refer to as crooked wire value, and this is what we will discuss next as we move from the specifics of sales excellence to the larger arena of business excellence.

PART 5

BUSINESS EXCELLENCE: FIND SOMETHING YOU DO WELL AND PERFECT IT

MANTRAS FOR EXCELLENCE:

O Crooked wire value results from the provision of innovative products and services (solutions) that are unexpected by the customer and unmatched by the competition.

O Three years from now, what is it that your market and your clients will be dying to have? Figure that one out and success will soon follow.

O The best brands don't wear out; they wear in.

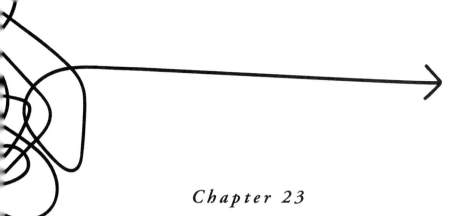

Chapter 23

CROOKED WIRE VALUE

I have a whiteboard in my office. I use it for a variety of lists and in meetings, but the two most common uses are as a kind of doodle pad to help me make and illustrate points when speaking with a team member or a client and as a visual device to remind me of our *priorities*. The illustration I turn to most often and that sometimes stays on my whiteboard for months at a time is a simple human stick figure with an arrow entering one side of the round body and exiting the other side of the body. The drawing is not glamorous, but the arrow is true to form in that it has a point on one end and fletching on the other end, so it at least looks like a real arrow. However, the arrow is not straight. In fact, it has about five or six ninety-degree bends in the section of the shaft that is inside the stick figure's body. The arrow is a way to illustrate a concept called crooked wire value that I learned about from a CEO I met in New York City during a meeting a few years back. The stick figure with the crooked arrow through it is the prop I have used for a long time to illustrate the ideal approach to value creation and value delivery.

"CROOKED WIRE VALUE"

Here is how it works. The stick figure represents any particular customer or a class of customers. If a straight arrow with a small shaft and a small point (not a broadhead) were to penetrate someone's abdomen, the real possibility exists that it might miss all vital organs and do minimal damage—or it might not. You might be able to simply pull it out, treat and bandage the puncture wounds, and live to fight another day. My aim when presenting this illustration is to help business leaders understand that if our value proposition is straight and clean and commoditized, almost undifferentiated from our competition's, then the customer may be able to simply extract us from their business without any major consequences, damage, or disruption and easily replace us with another straight arrow that fills the hole, stops the bleeding, and takes our place. By contrast, if my *crooked* arrow were embedded in someone's abdomen, when someone tried to remove it, all those crooks and bends are going to get caught up on organs and bones, and it's going to be hard to get out.

Now I'm not suggesting that we try to kill our customers by impaling them with arrows! Rather, our objective when competing in any market is to provide solutions that are not simply different from those provided by our competitors, but ones that deliver better results. We do that through the application of intelligent innovation that delivers measurable value via counterintuitive approaches. We encourage our team members to conceptualize and propose improvements and enhancements to our product and service offerings that meet three criteria:

- The improvement needs to deliver something of real value to the customer. It needs to enable the customer to operate their business more productively and more profitably.

- The product, service, feature, or function needs to be unmatched by the competition. In other words, whatever value we want to add must be either *unavailable* on the market, *not very well known or publicized,* or *accessible to only a few market participants* because of price or scarcity.

- The feature or function needs to be unexpected by the customer (they never saw it coming!).

Every time you embed an improvement in your solution suite that meets all three of these criteria, it is akin to putting a ninety-degree bend in the shaft of the arrow. What happens when you put enough bends in the arrow? The customer can no longer pull your company or your solutions out of their business because it would impede their ability to operate. How do you know when the solutions and improvements you are proposing meet the criteria for crooked wire value? Easy. The customer's response will be something like "Wow! We never thought of that, but that is exactly what we need!"

The indelible lesson seared into my business brain when I fully grasped the importance and impact of crooked wire value is this: The consistent delivery of crooked wire value makes it difficult, if not impossible, for our customers to defect—even when we are the more expensive option.

Our objective when competing in any market is to provide solutions that are not simply different from those provided by our competitors, but ones that deliver better results.

Why? Because our customers are addicted to our solutions and are not willing to live without them. Is there any greater competitive edge that we could achieve? I think not. Crooked wire value results from the provision of innovative products and services (solutions) that are unexpected by the customer and unmatched by the competition.

The challenge is this: In today's modern business climate with easy and open access to all technologies, market research and intelligence, a global supply base, etc., other than scope and scale, it can be difficult to differentiate one product, service, or business from another. Customers have come to demand quality regardless of where or from whom they procure the product. Product quality is a non-negotiable. As a result, it is difficult to create any long-term market and customer loyalty with product quality, even when fully embracing product innovation. The playing field of product quality has become virtually universally level across most industries, largely because all producers are using many of the same suppliers, raw materials, components, systems, cloud infrastructure, and other similarities.

Business today isn't like fine dining, where a world-class chef can literally make the same dish taste more delectable than the line cook down the street using the same ingredients. Think of it in this concrete way: I've already referred to my appreciation for well-engineered vehicles, many of them of German origin, as historically many of those luxury brands have touted quality and performance metrics that positioned them in a different echelon when compared to car brands that might be considered more common. However, the reality today is that nearly all automobile manufacturers are producing vehicles of high quality that don't look or perform radically different from the iconic brands that built their reputations on performance and/or quality. It's true that no one is going to mistake a Kia for a BMW, yet in terms of quality (and consumer expectations of quality), those two brands are not nearly as far apart as they were twenty years ago, and many of the creature comforts are similar even if their price tags are not. Here's another common scenario. When I purchase an appliance, regardless of where I purchase it—Amazon, a discount warehouse, a home improvement store, or a big box retailer—my expectations relative to quality, performance, and service are the same, and I expect an ability to return it with relative ease should I need to do so. Even though the brand or model number may be different based upon the sales outlet from which I purchased the item, it's literally the same manufacturer and the same product.

If product quality has been leveled across the global marketplace, the same cannot be said of service quality. The quality of service runs the gamut across all commercial sectors. This was made quite apparent to me on a trip I took to Korea a number of years ago and the eye-opening process of reentering my home country. South Korea is widely known for its friendly, consumer-focused customer service, where virtually every kind of retail operation is well staffed with smiling employees who make it a point to greet you and who are truly enthusiastic about offering assistance or answering questions. Free samples are common and tend to grow in number the more you spend. Frequently, sample products are physically attached as giveaways to products with which customers are already familiar as a way to introduce the consumer to new products and experiences. While providing free samples is not necessarily a novel way to introduce or market products, it demonstrates appreciation for customers' patronage. The general approach in Korea is to provide the customer with more than they expect and to demonstrate tremendous respect for them by being helpful and courteous. In fact, some Westerners are so shocked by the attention they receive from employees that they find it unnerving. That's because we are conditioned to a very different model of customer service, one where we are accustomed to employees whose demeanor in some cases suggests that customers are a nuisance. On my return from Korea, I was somewhat taken aback by the abrupt nature of the service professionals who manage the intake of citizens, residents, and visitors entering our country. I'd left Seoul amid a multitude of smiles, courteous expressions of thanks, and friendly waves. The Korean Air flight attendants seemed to genuinely care about the passengers' comfort. In the United States, we have become desensitized to mediocre customer service to the point that it brightens our day when we receive exemplary service. Think about the companies that routinely deliver customer experiences that exceed expectations and the loyalty their customers pay them. Perhaps your own list might match the top ten companies for customer service as ranked by the American Customer Satisfaction Index (ACSI), which, in 2018, for the first time broke with its tradition of providing only scorecards by industry category and released a list for all the companies it assesses:

Chick-fil-A, Trader Joe's, Aldi, Amazon, Lexus, Costco Wholesale, HEB Grocery, Toyota, Publix, and Wegmans Food Markets. ACSI is the only national cross-industry measure of customer satisfaction in the United States. It ranks companies within their industry based upon customer evaluations of the quality of goods and services purchased in America and produced by domestic and foreign firms with substantial US market shares.[9]

You might recognize that one of the companies on this list—Toyota—is one often highlighted for achieving organizational excellence because of their commitment to process through their adherence to the Toyota Production System (TPS), which created a purposeful mechanism for analyzing the current state, asking what it wanted to achieve by identifying the ideal state, and then building a step-by-step plan for how they would get from where they were to where they wanted to be. A central factor in their successful arrival at the where-we-want-to-be state was always applying their principle of Plan, Do, Check, Act (PDCA). Sound familiar? It's very similar in approach to the four As model of adopt, adapt, apply, and adjust that I covered earlier. The challenge that Toyota highlighted is that most of us have a product plan, but we don't have a plan for world-class service or continuous improvement.

Some companies do not place requisite importance on customer service. Some view it as too costly. Some just take it for granted—the fatality of assumptions about how leaders view their companies versus how their teams do—if they don't make a concerted effort to build an intentional culture. When it comes to product, technology has leveled the playing field, and many of us have to rely on straight arrows in our

9   Christopher Elliot, "These Companies Have the Best Customer Service," *Forbes*, July 11, 2018, https://www.forbes.com/sites/christopherelliott/2018/07/11/these-companies-have-the-best-customer-service-heres-why/?sh=6fca8ba0b80a.

product and service value propositions. Customer service presents an ideal canvas for brand differentiation. If we commit to conceptualize, create, and deliver unique and creative solutions in our services delivery model that provide an unexpected and unmatched experience for our customers, we achieve an advantage that is hard for the competition to combat.

Exceptional customer service can be a significant revenue generator, even when there is no revenue that is directly attributable to customer service. Giving customers a complete, cohesive experience that aligns with an organization's purpose makes people wholeheartedly buy into the brand, not just a particular product or product line. The truth is that exemplary customer service costs you nothing because of the boomerang effect. Much like a boomerang—your customers keep coming back!

What's the best way to fully capitalize on the boomerang effect? Let's look at crooked wire value in full context. To do so, I need to talk about another graphic I'm likely to draw on my whiteboard: a small box inside a large box. The smaller inner box represents the totality of all of our implicit customer commitments; this is the execution box. Every customer commitment inside that box must be executed/delivered in an accurate, complete, and timely manner. When you build an organization that understands how to consistently execute and deliver on all implicit commitments represented by the inner box, you can venture into the outer, larger box, which is all about expanding your role and impact beyond expectations—i.e., the generation and delivery of crooked wire value.

HOW SHOULD WE VIEW OUR ROLE AND RESPONSIBILITIES?

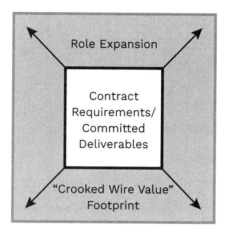

Don't just **support** or **serve** the client …
LEAD the client!
Expand our role … deliver additional unexpected business value …
make it virtually impossible for the client to defect!

Even with your long-term customers, you can never be over-confident. The political realm provides an ample metaphor. Rather than celebrating and letting your guard down because you have just won the election, it will serve you well to stay vigilant and behave as if you are still running for office. You have to ask yourself the following questions: "What services can we offer that will guarantee that our customers come back again and again (and ideally, never leave)?" "What can we deliver that no one else has?" "What can we legitimately claim that no other firm can claim without calling their credibility and integrity into question?" "How can we personalize our offerings to our customers' needs?" The only way to stay ahead in this game is to regularly ask yourself not only what will benefit your customer today but also three years from now, what is it that your market and your clients will be dying to have? Figure that one out and success will soon follow.

Think about FedEx's tagline slogan from the 1970s when it was a fledgling organization, the iconic "When it absolutely, positively has to be there overnight." The slogan, precisely because it wasn't just a slogan but a promise on which they consistently executed, helped FedEx separate itself from its competitors. That customer service expectation behind the slogan became their identity, one that proved to have staying power, for despite plenty of competition, when it comes to overnight delivery, small package focus, and sensitive, timely document management, FedEx still dominates the market. It got there by identifying what it could provide customers that no one else at the time was doing and then doing it better than anyone else. FedEx is a good example of how the best brands don't wear out; they wear in.

> If you want to achieve a competitive advantage, start by really understanding your customer, their values, their needs, and how they wish to position themselves for the future. Then figure out what you can offer them that is in keeping with what they value, fulfills their needs, and sets them up for future success.

If you want to achieve a competitive advantage, start by really understanding your customer, their values, their needs, and how they wish to position themselves for the future. Then figure out what you can offer them that is in keeping with what they value, fulfills their needs, and sets them up for future success. What can you offer them that no one else can, no one else will, or no one else has thought of?

That's your crooked wire value. Then execute on what you promise. If you can't execute, then your crooked wire isn't a wire at all; it's just a wet noodle.

MANTRAS FOR EXCELLENCE:

O   My ultimate business objective? To work myself into a position of irrelevance and obscurity.

Chapter 24

DECISION-MAKING
BY THE NUMBERS

I discovered many years ago that good leadership creates for its followers an environment that is the perfect balance of empowerment and accountability. Empowerment devoid of accountability is anarchy, and accountability devoid of true empowerment and authority begets paralysis. The challenge of creating this type of organizational paradigm is greatest when trying to migrate or transform an organization from a centralized leadership model to a distributed one when the organization has been ruled for many years by a single dynamic entrepreneur, leader, or autocrat, many times the founder of the business. Over the years, when I have stepped into the top role in a number of midsize companies, I recognized the need to establish a more decentralized decision-making and leadership

> Good leadership creates for its followers an environment that is the perfect balance of empowerment and accountability.

model to accelerate operational maturity and growth. However, in several environments in which we have initiated such a transformation, we were challenged to achieve transformational change because the existing leadership team or newly appointed leaders failed to adopt the mantle of leadership because they simply did not believe that the change in the leadership approach was real. The result in many cases was a mirage of change, resulting in no material improvements in operational and/or financial performance, and worse, a complete stall in leadership development and leadership distribution.

As I encountered this reality in a number of companies where I have worked, it dawned on me that organizations need a simple conceptual framework that helps leaders clearly understand the reach and limits of their leadership and decision-making authority and enables them to more easily gauge which decisions they can and should make unilaterally and which ones deserve and demand outside perspective and input. Faced with that challenge, I crafted a simple three-step decision-making model that has worked for more than twenty-five years and is just as applicable today as it was the day that it was conceived. It has proven to be easy to understand and just as easy to implement and execute. I call this process the 3-2-1 decision-making model.

3. When facing any decision, there are *three boundaries* that we do not breach. These three boundaries are off-limits by rule. A rule has borders that are hard and fast and nonnegotiable, and if you break a rule, you are in peril of losing your job. The three boundaries and the rule that applies will sound familiar, for it is the same one that I illuminated at the beginning of the book relative to personal behavior and must, under this leadership approach, extend to the entire organization: The rule is this: We will not take any action or

engage in any activity that is illegal, immoral, or unethical, and we won't get close to anything that may be perceived as such. If anyone affiliated with the business is faced with any opportunity or choice that in any way smells of illegality, immorality, or unethicality, the decision is swift and definitive; the answer is always no.

2. Our behavior as leaders needs to adhere to *two* guidelines. Guidelines are a little fuzzier than rules, and they are more open to interpretation, but they are not difficult to understand. In short, a leader's behavior, both at work and away from work, should reflect and reinforce our brand values and brand culture. If it does not, then we confuse the buying public, and we either vacate our brand equity, or worse, we erode it. When we behave ethically and predictably and in concert with our brand values and culture, those around us place their trust in us. When they need the types of products and services that we sell, they naturally transfer that trust to the organization we represent. And remember, trust is at the foundation of all long-term personal and business relationships.

1. Lastly, when a decision needs to be made, and it has to be made *quickly*, how do I know which decisions I can make on my own and which decisions require additional counsel and guidance? We teach our leaders at all levels to ask themselves, "Is the decision that needs to be made of such a magnitude that, were I to be wrong, it would catastrophically or irreparably damage one or more of the six Cs?"

- Our *company*

- An important *customer*

- A significant *contract*

- My *confidence*

- My *character*

- Our company's *culture*

If the risk is low, make the decision. As long as you don't destroy one or more of the six Cs, executive leadership has your back regardless of whether you are right or wrong. If the decision proves to be wrong, then that decision has not harmed anything of an irreplaceable or mission-critical nature, and we can recover. And being wrong relative to a decision of a manageable magnitude actually provides a teaching moment and

> **If the risk is low, make the decision.**

moves us one step closer to the right answer because it eliminates a wrong one. If the risk is significant, seek additional counsel. Get someone else in the boat with you before making the decision. In short, when making a decision that shows little propensity to destroy one or more of these six Cs, our leaders are fully empowered.

Over many years and in a number of companies, the deployment of the 3-2-1 decision-making model has resulted in the development of better, wiser, more mature leaders—faster. And that leaves more time for me to accomplish my ultimate business objective: to work myself into a position of irrelevance and obscurity and fade into the background gracefully.

MANTRAS FOR EXCELLENCE:

- "Don't stop when you're tired; stop when you're done." —David Goggins

- Many times, the things we want to do the least are the things we ought to do the most.

- "Never make peace with a weakness." —Jimmy Fowler

- When is the best time to fire somebody? The first time you think about it."

- Life never turns out exactly like you want. What you get is not always what you choose. Plan accordingly.

- No battle plan survives unscathed first contact with the enemy.

- "Next to love, balance is the most important thing." —John Wooden

Chapter 25

MANY TIMES, THE THINGS WE *WANT* TO DO THE LEAST ARE THE THINGS WE *OUGHT* TO DO THE MOST

Since the early 2000s, I have carried a Moleskine notebook small enough to slip into my shirt or pants pocket. I use it every day without fail. In it I keep my daily to-do list, and uniquely, my to-do list is never more than eleven items each day. Why only eleven tasks in a day? Well, first, the size of the Moleskine notebook that I use has twenty-two lines on each page, and I bisect each page by drawing a horizontal boundary below line eleven on each page. I then put the date in the upper right-hand corner of each of the two sections on each page so that each page carries my to-do's for two consecutive days. Thus, the size of the notebook and the number of lines on each page are a factor in the size limit of my daily task list. But the other reason is more important. Most of our to-do lists are way too long and are unrealistic. When our daily task list is too long, it creates frustration because it feels as if we are never making significant progress toward accomplishing the things that we *think* need to get done. I try to be a little more realistic when planning each day.

Throughout the day as needs become apparent or visible, I write down things that I know I need to do in the future on the appropriate page that corresponds to that future date, so the book usually carries my plans for the next few weeks, and items get added to various pages throughout the week. I put only Monday through Friday dates in the book, and I omit weekends and holidays. Fridays are reserved for personal tasks that I want to accomplish over the weekend, and I leave some room (three to four lines) on Fridays for overflow business items that for whatever reason I failed to complete Monday through Thursday. I also use Fridays for researching potential suppliers or partners and new services, solutions, and technologies being introduced in our industry. But the key to the book's effectiveness is this: Every morning, I open the book to that day's half page of to-do's, and I ask myself two important questions. The first question is, "What are the three things that I absolutely *without fail* must complete today that, whether anybody knows about them or not, will make the biggest difference in the operational and financial performance of this company?" I highlight those three things with a yellow highlighter. The second question is similar: "What is the ONE thing that I absolutely *without fail* must complete today that, whether anybody knows about it or not, will make the biggest difference in my faith, my family, and my friendships?" Again, I highlight that "to-do" item with a yellow highlighter. My two questions seek to identify those things that I need to *complete*, not just work on. The focus is on getting the truly important stuff done. And done well.

By faithfully executing this system, I know at a glance which activities, tasks, and initiatives top my priority list every day. I write each list in full knowledge that nearly all my days meet with interruptions and emergencies requiring my attention that many times keep me from accomplishing everything that I planned, so those may get dragged forward to a future day based upon their level of importance. But I *always* do my absolute best to *complete* the items highlighted in yellow. Sometimes that makes for some long days. But as once stated by the ultramarathoner, triathlete, and author David Goggins, "Don't stop when you're tired; stop when you're done."

Prioritizing that list is one of the first things I do each day. Looking at the list before me offers the reminder that many times, the things we *want* to do the least are the things we *ought* to do the most. That's as true in life as it is at work. In my estimation, it's wise to get these tough things done at the top of the day. Difficult tasks require fortitude, commitment, willpower, and resolve. Difficult decisions are not supposed to be easy, and they're certainly not fun. But they have to be carried out. My experience is that many of the difficult decisions that I have to make are people decisions. Those are always the hardest decisions, even when we know what we need to do. My first two rules of being a CEO or a president are (1) protect the interests of the shareholders, and (2) ensure the financial viability and vitality of the organization. To accomplish those two objectives, I can't protect individual team members, especially those who are underperforming, as I have committed to put the performance and health of the overall organization first. I can't give a pass to any particular

> **Difficult tasks require fortitude, commitment, willpower, and resolve.**

employee at the expense of the company, as the company is what I have committed to preserve and protect. It is easy to drag our feet on those tough people decisions and to tell ourselves that we will deal with it next week. But two mantras come to mind that always push me to do the right thing—the hard thing—sooner rather than later. A great friend and local Greenville banker, Jimmy Fowler, taught me this principle: Never make peace with a weakness. The second mantra or principle sounds somewhat harsh and crass, but there is a lot of truth in it: When is the best time to fire somebody? The first time you think about it.

So it's best to hit the hard things while your mind is relatively uncluttered and before others begin to make demands on your time that compromise your ability to accomplish the truly important objectives. I believe that all leaders benefit from regimens that allow them some quiet time first thing in their day to engage in uninterrupted thought and then from that time apply critical thinking in the form of planning. Using my notebook, I can rationally plan and prioritize my day, with a nod toward the following reality: Life never turns out exactly like you want. What you get is not always what you choose. Plan accordingly. How? Figure out your priorities—in your day, in your business, and in your life—while leaving a little wiggle room for adjustment when unexpected, but genuine, priorities appear on the horizon.

When you learn how to prioritize, which means really scrutinizing the professional and personal to-do's that make up your list for each day, an overarching theme for me is identifying those items or activities that hold the potential to make the biggest impact in the lives of other people. Even if that means terminating an employee and then helping them find a place and a role in which they can truly succeed, it is about making others' lives better. The immediate effect may be unpleasant, but the long-term objective is to help people get to where they need to be so that they can be productive and fulfilled.

By identifying what needs to be completed *now*—especially the hard things on which it would be easy to procrastinate—you can form a priority list for attack, albeit one that is agile enough to meet inevitably changing needs. Form your priorities, plan an approach to accomplishing them as best as you are able, then be prepared to adapt. Remember, no battle plan survives unscathed first contact with the enemy.

Prioritization for me ultimately is about ensuring that my job and the things that I do meet the test of what I call the five Fs of work. I share with others that the measure of an ideal job is that it provides enough ("enough" varies by individual) level of the following: *financial* reward and *free* time (if the job pays richly but consumes virtually all my waking hours, then my job is my life, which is not good) so that we can invest both in the things that really matter, our *faith*, our *families*, and our *friends*.

Following the five Fs allows us to live by John Wooden's essential quote: "Next to love, balance is the most important thing." If you can create balance in your life, you will discover that there is no force that can stop you from achieving both personal and professional success and significance.

> **If you can create balance in your life, you will discover that there is no force that can stop you from achieving both personal and professional success and significance.**

MANTRAS FOR EXCELLENCE:

O   Be present.

O   We all have a timeline; we just don't live like we have a
    timeline. Face reality; live like today may be your last.

O   There is plenty of sunshine to go around. Make sure
    you let others stand in the brightest spot sometimes.

O   You don't choose a life; you live one.

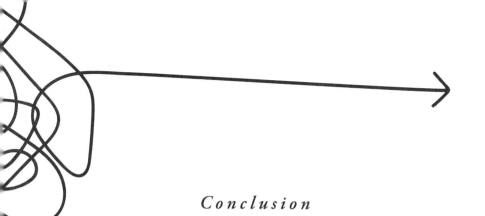

BE PRESENT

This book is my attempt at sharing what my life and work have taught me about trying to be my best self, the best leader I'm capable of being, and doing my part to lead businesses that consistently strive for excellence. As you've seen, some of the roads I've traveled in my pursuit of excellence have been smooth, some have even featured curbs and guardrails that protected me and kept me out of the ditch, and others have been riddled with potholes and washboard ruts. However, they have all taught me something valuable and allowed me to crystallize those essential characteristics of authentic leaders that enable them to create sustainable, positive, productive cultures in the organizations they help lead. Along the way, I learned that none of us are ever going to be excellent leaders or run outstanding businesses if we don't know precisely who we are and what we value. If you've stayed with me this far, you have a decent idea about both of those things relative to my own life. I've been around long enough to know that I'm always going to fall a bit short of the lofty ideals I set, but the target is still excellence—in reality, perfection. Perfection is unachievable, but it is still an admirable goal. To come as close as we are capable to achieving excellence or perfection means never giving up. You have to press on, knowing when to zig and when to zag, but you can't quit. As Randy Dobbs, my good friend and author of the book *Transformational Leadership* said, "If you quit, you can't win." I'm hopeful that this thought and the other mantras in this book that were discovered by myself and others in pursuit of excellence might help you get closer to achieving it as well.

We accomplish excellence—in our teams, in our businesses, in our relationships—by first becoming mindful of who we are and what we expect of ourselves. To achieve excellence requires that we be present and live every moment as fully as we can. We all have a timeline; we just don't live like we have a timeline. Face reality; live today like it may be your last. I genuinely enjoy going to work each day. I enjoy the collaborative and creative energy of working with others. I have a passion for teaching. I enjoy finding ways to overcome obstacles, improve performance, and accomplish something I thought was just outside the reach of our capabilities, competencies, and capacity. I still experience a thrill at closing a challenging and complex sale. As I have gotten older, I find passion and communion among my family and my friends and in my faith

> We accomplish excellence—in our teams, in our businesses, in our relationships—by first becoming mindful of who we are and what we expect of ourselves.

that consumes a greater share of my attention and thought as I have given away more of my professional responsibilities to the next generation of leaders who deserve the chance to be the difference makers. It is their time to stand in the spotlight. I penned a short three-page piece a few years ago titled "Essential Elements for Success and Significance in Business and in Life." It contains only thirteen salient points, but one of them is this: There is plenty of sunshine to go around. Make sure you let others stand in the brightest spot sometimes. That's where I find myself today in my business endeavors, but I have also tried to demonstrate that sort of humility along the journey. Humility is one of the core traits of an authentic leader, and I hope that I have not failed in genuinely putting others first.

I hope that you have found helpful some of the mantras that have been the focus of this book. I also hope that by reading about the ideas and philosophies that have guided my approach to leadership you will be inspired to architect your own values-based framework of mantras that shape first how you think and then how you behave. By being a living model of the principles and values that are at the core of your nature, you will create consistency in your patterns of decision-making and predictability for how you treat others. That in turn will increase the level of trust placed in you by those surrounding you and expand your sphere of influence. We need more good leaders. Be one. While I don't know the origin of this quotation, it is one I have always loved and try to remember: You don't choose a life; you live one. Why not live yours to its fullest? When you do, excellence will be the outcome.

> **We need more good leaders. Be one.**

About the Author

G. T. "Toby" Stansell continues to serve in executive leadership roles for high-impact, fast-growth organizations that want to leverage innovation and technology for improved performance. Toby possesses an innate ability to develop and deploy innovative approaches to an organization's most pressing challenges, and his leadership infuses an indelible culture within commercial, civic, and cultural entities that motivates, galvanizes, and unifies the organization's personnel to fulfill its true purpose. Toby's primary objectives when leading an organization are to impart a sustainable positive and productive culture, identify and capitalize upon transformative opportunities, and optimize efficiencies and financial performance.

Toby is the chief executive officer of Cargo, LLC, a business strategy and marketing consultancy that helps big brands more effectively market and sell to small to medium businesses. Immediately prior to assuming the CEO position at Cargo, in January 2021, Toby served as a principal with Cherry Bekaert's Digital Advisory Service Line. Before joining Cherry Bekaert, Toby served as president and chief operating officer of Acumen IT, LLC. Toby came to Acumen after achieving his first presidential role with OOBE, Inc., after rising through senior sales and marketing roles at IBM, Jobscope Corporation, Right Source, Western Data Systems, and Factory Logic.

A graduate of Clemson University, Toby has taught leadership courses there and through the Greenville Chamber's Minority Business Accelerator. Among a long history of extensive volunteer work with the Greenville Chamber, he served on the Chamber Board of Directors for nine years, the Strategic Cabinet as vice chair of economic competitiveness for seven years, and as cochair of the Accelerate! Greenville economic development initiative for eleven years.